RELIGION
IN MINUTES

DISCARD

MARCUS WEEKS

RELIGION
IN MINUTES

MARCUS WEEKS

Quercus

CONTENTS

Introduction   6
Religious belief and practice   8
Indigenous traditional religions   28
Ancient religions   36
Zoroastrianism   66
Jainism   72
Hinduism   80
Buddhism   128
Religion in China and Japan   170

Judaism	190
Christianity	240
Islam	302
Sikhism	352
New religions and cults	370
Challenges to religion	398
Glossary	408
Index	412
Acknowledgements	416

Introduction

We live in an age dominated by science and technology, and by unprecedented material prosperity. Rationality and knowledge are prized and fostered in our societies, and the authority of religious institutions has declined so that today the overwhelming majority of nations pride themselves on being secular democracies. Yet despite this, an estimated two-thirds of the world's population readily describe themselves as religious.

It is not difficult to understand the apparent need we humans have for religious belief: when confronted with the immensity and complexity of the cosmos, and the 'miracle' of life, religion offers a framework for explaining and understanding mysteries that philosophy and science have not yet satisfactorily resolved.

Although today a majority of people identify with Christianity, Islam, Hinduism or Buddhism, there has been a rich variety of religions through the ages and in different parts of the world. Some are ancient, some now extinct, others recently established, and each has distinctive beliefs and practices, but the majority have several common features. Foremost of these is faith, a belief in something, usually a supernatural power, being or principle. It is this faith, rather than evidence-based rational explanation, that distinguishes religion from science and philosophy.

But religion is more than simply belief in something otherwise inexplicable. In an individual this would be thought of as faith or spirituality; religion implies a shared belief, involving communal activity, an institution, rituals and a moral code. Because a religion offers a comprehensive belief system, it often also provides a mythology about the origins of its people, and as such becomes a cornerstone of that society's culture.

As civilizations come and go, so too do their religions. But as with other parts of their cultures, religions do not simply disappear. Instead, they are assimilated into the cultures and belief systems that ostensibly replace them. Elements of many ancient religions survive to the present day, and perhaps centuries from now (although believers would be loath to concede it) many of today's religions will be seen as historical curiosities too, influencing the beliefs of a future age.

The natural world

Humans are by nature inquisitive. We have an apparent need to understand the world around us, and yet some things defy our attempts at rational explanation.

For prehistoric people, the Sun, Moon and stars seemed magical, literally other-worldly, and became associated with supernatural beings or spirits. The regular cycles of night and day, and the changing of the seasons, could be understood as the workings of these spirits and other natural phenomena, including seas, rivers and mountains; living things such as forests, plants and animals; and natural dangers such as storms, floods and droughts. All of these had, and still have, a profound effect on human life, providing nourishment or threatening existence. Even when civilization brought with it an increased philosophical and scientific understanding of the natural world, the miracles of life, death and the creation of the Universe remained mysterious. Religions continue to offer explanations for these mysteries, to make sense of the Universe and to search for meaning in life.

Creation stories

Religious explanations of the mysteries of the natural world almost invariably appear in story form, often as myths that personify both natural and supernatural forces such as the Sun, the oceans and the spark of life itself. Myths sometimes give a metaphorical description of the actions of certain spirits or gods, and how they affect our everyday lives.

Such mythology is a focal point of all cultures. The stories are well known within the community and form the basis of religion. As well as explaining natural phenomena, most religions also offer some description of the greatest natural mystery: how the Universe, and everything in it, came to be. There are many different versions of the Creation story. Some involve a supreme being who brings cosmic order out of chaos or nothingness, while others feature a union of male and female spirits. Others still describe an eternal Universe within which supernatural forces create life. Some religions also predict an end to the Unilverse, often associated with an apocalyptic battle.

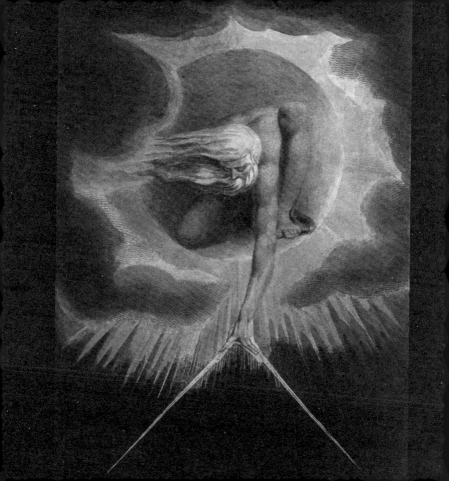

Supernatural beings

In describing the supernatural forces responsible for the creation of the cosmos, most religions focus on spirit beings that, more often than not, are personified as gods.

Most ancient and folk religions identify deities with specific objects, such as the Sun or Moon, but also with more abstract concepts that include fertility, love and war. Normally, these deities are eternal and therefore immortal. Since each natural phenomenon was associated with a particular deity, most ancient religions were polytheistic. Frequently, however, one of the gods became regarded as a supreme being – generally a Creator god – reigning over the others. Around 3,000 years ago, truly monotheistic religions began to appear in the civilizations of the Middle East, giving rise especially to the Abrahamic religions Judaism, Christianity and Islam. But even within these monotheistic religions, lesser supernatural beings such as angels are believed to exist, as well as an evil counterpart to the one benevolent God, such as Satan.

Souls and spirits

As well as providing explanations for those things that give and sustain life, religions also seek to satisfy our curiosity about what happens when we die. They offer reassurance that life on Earth is in preparation for an eternal afterlife.

In virtually every religion, there is a belief in a human soul or spirit that is separate and distinct from the physical body, and that lives on after death. Concepts of what happens to the soul after physical death differ from faith to faith. Many religions describe a place where these spirits go – a heavenly domain in which the god or gods reside or a subterranean realm of shades. Over time, the idea evolved that the nature of the eternal afterlife was dependent on the Earthly life of the deceased. Particularly in monotheistic religions the choice was a simple one: heavenly paradise or punitive hell. Other religions, especially Hinduism and Buddhism, do not envisage the after life as a destination, but as part of a journey on which the soul is reincarnated in a constant cycle of life, death and rebirth.

Honouring the gods

Since deities are credited as being the supernatural powers responsible for the natural world, they are generally regarded as superior to us mortals. It is unsurprising, then, that religions place great importance on showing respect and honour to the gods.

Religious practices include ceremonies of worship, praising the power of a god or gods and making votive offerings to them. In many ancient religions, this took the form of ritual sacrifice of an animal or even a human, or in dedicating a portion of the harvest or the hunt to the deity. In later religions, the offerings became more symbolic promises of devotion. A person may pledge to give up his or her life to religion or charitable work, or to pray for guidance in living the life that the god intended for them, and for forgiveness for any transgressions. In return, followers petition their gods for favours, asking for their assistance in their everyday lives, such as providing them with the basic necessities to survive and protecting them from natural disaster.

Mesoamerican Aztec religion incorporated human sacrifice to various gods, as recorded in this 16th-century codex.

Rituals and rites

While followers of a given religion can perform some kind of devotion at any time, it is normal to formalize these in ritual acts of communal worship. In addition to daily or weekly ceremonies, certain times of the year also have significance and are celebrated through festivals, feasts and fasts.

Common to most religions are rituals linked to the changing seasons, especially the important times of the agricultural calendar – the arrival of spring or harvest time – times at which followers seek divine intervention in fertility and productivity. Many religions commemorate elements of their mythology, too, such as the birth of prophets and saints' days. There are also personal milestones in an individual's life that are marked with religious rituals for divine approval. The birth of a child and funeral rituals are universally observed, and there are other rites of passage, such as initiation or coming-of-age ceremonies and the public taking of marriage vows, all of which are integral to many religions.

Russian women reconstruct an ancient Slavic ritual welcoming spring.

Sacred places

Just as the gods of ancient religions were identified with abstract concepts (see page 12), they were also frequently associated with features of the landscape. As well as there being gods of the sea or a river, for example, there were also specific places that were considered sacred – either as the home of a deity or as the site of some mythological event.

Forests, mountains and other geographical features might be assigned religious significance as the creations of a deity, while other places were chosen for astronomical reasons – for example, the very spot at which the Sun rises on an important day of the year, such as midsummer. Some of these places became sites for burial grounds or for structures and buildings in which to perform religious rituals. The tradition of having a building devoted to religious worship – a temple, church, synagogue or mosque, for example – is common to almost all faiths. These, along with shrines dedicated to holy people such as saints or prophets, can become the destination of pilgrimages.

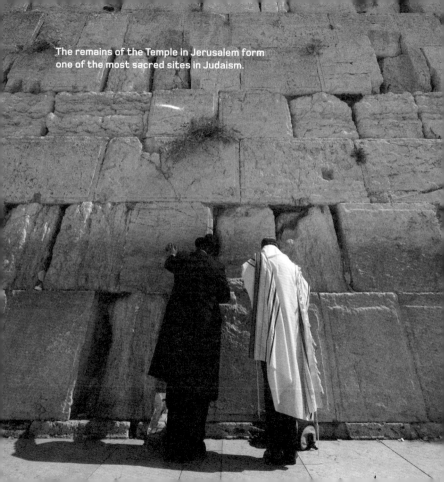

The remains of the Temple in Jerusalem form one of the most sacred sites in Judaism.

Holy people

A religion is generally a social institution that has a structure within the society in which it exists. More often than not, there is a hierarchy with a class of spiritual leaders, or priests, who may be elders of the community, scholars and teachers of religious knowledge or conductors of religious rituals.

While not actually worshipped, these figures are respected members of the community, giving moral as well as spiritual guidance. They may be chosen for their wisdom or, as in the case of shamans (see page 32), for their ability to act as intermediaries between the people and the gods or spirits. Some are particularly revered as prophets – bringing the word of their god as it has been revealed to them – or as saints or semi-divine beings with some supernatural quality, such as performing miracles. In many societies, there is a tradition of monasticism, a class of people who devote their lives entirely to their religion. These holy men and women – monks and nuns – renounce secular society and concentrate on prayer, worship and charitable work.

Good and evil

In providing explanations for the mysteries of life and the Universe, religions generally describe good and evil spirits that influence the world in which we live. Implicit in these are the very concepts of 'good' and 'evil' and right and wrong.

More explicitly, religions offer a system of morality, either in the form of guidelines for the correct way to live one's life, such as the Buddhist Eightfold Path (see page 144), or rules that constitute unacceptable behaviour, such as the Ten Commandments of Judaism and Christianity (see page 196). There are remarkable similarities among the moral codes of most religions, often based on some variant of the so-called golden rule, 'do as you would be done by', where actions that include killing, stealing and lying are almost universally prohibited. Other codes are specific to certain religions, especially those concerning sexual relationships or hygiene and food. Many things that are forbidden by a religion are based on experience – the prohibition of certain foods to avoid food poisoning, for example.

Religion and society

A defining feature of a religion is that it is a communal activity. Generally speaking, an individual with his or her own spiritual beliefs may be considered as religious, but not part of a religion. To be recognized as a religion, those beliefs need to be systematically organized, and shared by others. And because religions consist of shared beliefs, and almost invariably communal observance in the form of ceremonies or rituals, they play an important social as well as spiritual role.

The act of worship, for example, is a community activity that brings together people with a common purpose. At a local level, the temple or church can be as much a social as a religious centre of a community; from a wider perspective, a religion can be closely connected to national or regional identity. Religious rituals often involve music and dancing that are central to a society's cultural heritage, and the mythology – sometimes formalized as holy scriptures – is often an important influence on a society's literature or ties in with its history.

In Polynesian societies, a meeting house called the 'marae' is the focus of religious and social life.

Traditional beliefs

A number of traditional religions have survived into the modern era, mainly in parts of the world that have remained untouched by industrialized society. Indigenous peoples in Africa, South America, Australasia and even parts of North America and the more remote areas of Europe and Asia, maintain belief systems and religious rituals that have existed in an unbroken tradition going back, sometimes, for thousands of years.

Unlike the ancient religions of, for example, Egypt and Greece, or still-flourishing ancient faiths such as Hinduism, these are not the religious expressions of civilizations, but of smaller, and generally less sophisticated, tribal communities. As such, they can help to give an insight into the beliefs and practices of prehistoric cultures. With the rapid advances in communication technology in today's globalized world, many of these 'folk religions' have come under threat as their followers have contact with modern society, but in some areas, such as the American Northwest, there has been a concerted effort to preserve tradition.

Totem poles commemorate the history and mythology of many Native American tribes.

Animistic beliefs

The traditional indigenous religions that survive have a strong connection with the natural world. Whether within a nomadic, hunter-gatherer community or a more settled agricultural society, the way of life is intimately connected to the cycle of seasons and the animals and crops necessary for survival.

Many of these traditional religions are animistic and describe natural phenomena as possessing supernatural spirits. In some of these belief systems elements such as the Sun or the Moon are identified as gods, while in others everything in the natural world is an expression of a supreme god or creator. It is generally believed that these spirits and deities can be influenced by religious rituals and appeased by sacrifices from the hunt or harvest. Many of these religions reflect a symbiotic relationship between people and their environment and believe that, in return for the goods nature provides, the gods expect people to do their work as stewards of the natural world, living in harmony with nature rather than exploiting it.

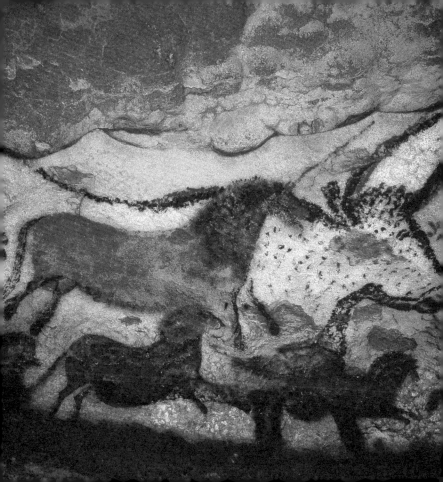

Spirit worlds

There is a tendency among indigenous people leading traditional lifestyles to believe in other worlds – places that are separate from the world we know, and that are inhabited by good and evil spirits or the souls of deceased ancestors.

In common with other religions, such communities may hold ceremonies and rituals in a attempt to communicate with the spirits, to ask for their assistance in the hunt or for a successful harvest, for example. But there are also those among them – shamans – who are believed to have an innate ability to contact the spirits. They can act as intermediaries between their communities and the spirits, and even visit spirit worlds when in a trance or dreamlike state, or under the influence of certain drugs. Shamans are found in traditional societies worldwide and are generally held to have additional powers, especially those of healing. The 'witch doctors' of many indigenous African religions and the 'medicine men' of the tribes of native North Americans are good examples of these.

A shaman of the Native American Koskimo tribe in British Columbia, Canada.

Survival of folk religions

Very few places in the world remain untouched by modern society. Many indigenous peoples have seen a traditional way of life all but disappear and their religions threatened – first by colonization and, later, by global trade and urbanization.

Some survive simply because of their remoteness (as with the highland tribes of Papua New Guinea), while others practise at least some of their old beliefs, despite pressure to modernize. Others still have adapted to the times, incorporating new ideas and influences from other religions in a new faith that nevertheless retains features of the original (see page 390). A few, however, have clung stubbornly to indigenous religions, sometimes out of resistance to change, but also as a conscious preservation of their culture. This is especially true of peoples once subjugated by colonization or forced to conform by political regimes. In recent years, a number of extinct or near-extinct folk religions, such as the ancient religions of Central America, have been revived as part of such nationalistic movements.

Warriors dance at the Goroka Sing-Sing, a traditional annual gathering in Papua New Guinea.

Mesopotamian religions

During the Bronze Age, nomadic peoples settled in the fertile land of Mesopotamia between the rivers Tigris and Euphrates. Their communities had a sophisticated social structure, in which a shared belief played an important role.

The Sumerians, who settled during the fourth millennium BCE, established several small kingdoms with a common religion. The mythology of their gods, such as the water god Enki and sky god Anu, was an integral part of Sumerian culture. The Babylonian people gradually superseded the Sumerians in the third millennium BCE, absorbing much of their religion. They added gods of their own, the most important of whom was Marduk, the son of Enki, who was given the power to organize the Universe. The metaphor of a Babylonian god emerging from Sumerian origins was part of the epic *Enuma Elis*, a Creation myth that helped to legitimize Babylonian rule. The Babylonians were conquered in 691 BCE by the Assyrians, who similarly adapted Babylonian mythology, replacing Marduk with their god, Ashur.

Ninurta, a Mesopotamian god of war and hunting

Religion in ancient Egypt

Stretching along the river Nile, the kingdom of ancient Egypt brought together several different peoples under the rule of its pharaohs. The success of this civilization, lasting from about 3100 to 323 BCE, depended largely on the ability of the pharaohs to absorb local cultures and integrate various beliefs into one common religion as they acquired their territory.

To support their power, they claimed to be god-kings, the sons of Ra, the Sun god, and developed a mythology linking themselves to local gods. As this Egyptian religion evolved, various principal deities emerged. The most important of these was Osiris, originally a fertility god of the people of Lower Egypt. Osiris was drowned by his brother Set, the evil god of the desert, but his body was rescued by his sister Isis, and made immortal by embalming. Coupling with her brother's remains, Isis conceived the god of the sky, Horus (opposite). Consequently, Osiris acquired an almost equal status to Ra, as god of life and death and ruler of the afterlife, while Isis took on the role of the mother goddess.

The Egyptian afterlife

Through the claim that they were descendants of Ra, Egyptian pharaohs were perceived as being immortal. The idea of an afterlife was initially restricted to the god-kings, but developed into a cult of immortality that was available to the nobility, too. To ensure the *ka* (soul) lived on in the afterlife, the body was mummified – in imitation of the embalming of Osiris – and buried with essential grave goods and statues of servants.

Funeral rituals were followed scrupulously, and instructions for the correct procedures – collections of texts known as The Book of the Dead – were often entombed with the mummified bodies. These describe scenes such as the jackal-headed Anubis escorting the deceased to a place of judgement in the realm of Osiris, to decide whether or not they are fit for immortality. In this ceremony, the heart of the dead person is weighed against a feather of Ma'at, the god of justice, and if successful, the deceased is taken to join Osiris and Isis among the other immortal gods.

Chinese mythology

As the Chinese people adopted a settled agricultural lifestyle and laid foundations for the great Chinese civilization, they inherited a religious tradition from their tribal ancestors.

Ancient Chinese religions were largely animistic, identifying natural phenomena with deities. From these emerged gods such as the supreme deity Shangdi, later known as *Tian* (heaven), represented as a dragon, and *Di* (Earth), represented as a phoenix. Shamans (see page 32) also played a role in these traditional Chinese religions, communicating with the spirit world and with the souls of dead ancestors. From the 3rd millennium BCE, China gradually became a unified empire, and religion was an essential ingredient in creating social cohesion. As in other civilizations, mythology mingled with history, providing a framework for Chinese society, as in the legend of the Jade emperor, the first god or 'heavenly grandfather', and the model for dynastic rule. Emperors were regarded as the descendants of the gods, embodying not only their power but also their virtues, and with a divine right to rule.

Dragons play an important role in Chinese mythology, and were often seen as symbols of imperial power.

Yin and yang

Most traditional Chinese religions ascribe the creation of the Universe not to a creator god, but as a consequence of the tension between two cosmic forces: *Tian* (heaven) and *Di* (Earth). These are analogous to the attributes of the dragon and the phoenix, male and female, action and receptiveness, light and dark. As such, they symbolize the essential duality of the cosmos that lies at the heart of much Chinese thought.

In later Chinese philosophy, these forces were characterized as 'yin', the passive principle associated with waning, and 'yang', the active principle associated with growth. Other key concepts common to ancient Chinese beliefs also helped to shape the religious philosophy of the Chinese Empire, with its emphasis on human society and its place in the cosmos rather than on the worship of deities. Foremost of these are the concepts of *Tian* as the divine source of morality and the life force *Qi*, which gives energy to every living thing. Other ideas concern the organization of everyday life based on divine example.

Greek gods

The pantheon of ancient Greek gods evolved as Greek civilization absorbed the beliefs of various peoples in the first millennium BCE, creating a complex hierarchy with three distinct generations of gods. Minoan Crete provided a Creation myth telling how Gaia, the Earth, gave birth to a race of Titans fathered by Ouranos, the Sky. Among these were Cronus and Rhea, parents of Zeus.

In the Greek adaptation of this myth, Zeus became king of the present generation of gods, residing on Mount Olympus with his family entourage of siblings and cousins. Amongst the most important of these were Hera, goddess of women and the family; Poseidon, god of the sea; Demeter, goddess of fertility and the harvest; Athena, goddess of war and wisdom; Apollo, the Sun god and god of knowledge; Artemis, goddess of the Moon and hunting; Ares, god of war; Aphrodite, goddess of love and beauty; Hermes, the messenger of the gods; and Dionysus, god of the vine, wine and religious ecstasy. Zeus's brother Hades was also considered a major deity, but lived in his own kingdom, the underworld.

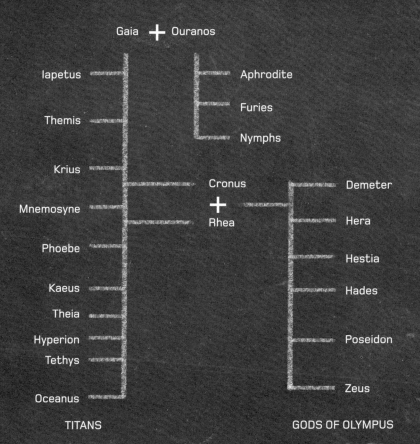

Myths and mortals

The Greek gods were not depicted as being all that different from the Greeks themselves. In tales of how the Olympians defeated the Titans, the gods show the same failings as humans – pride, greed and lust. They are not abstract concepts either, but had human forms and interacted with mortals, even to the extent of sexual liaisons producing semi-divine children.

What distinguished them from humans was their immortality, and the influence they had over natural phenomena and human affairs. The poet Hesiod's *Theogony* (*c.* 700 BCE) describes the emergence of this race of immortals and their complex relationships. Other epic poets, notably Homer in his *Iliad* and *Odyssey*, tell of the intervention of the gods in key moments of Greek history. By the time these myths were recorded, however, the degree to which the gods were actively involved in the world of humans had diminished considerably, and in the heyday of classical Greece, the immortals, although still a powerful influence, were believed mainly to confine themselves to their home on Mount Olympus.

The Judgement of Paris, by Peter Paul Rubens

Greek temples

Because of the mythical interaction between the gods and mortals, religion played an integral part in Greek public life. The gods were often consulted through the medium of oracles for their advice, as much for matters of state as personal problems. The most famous of these was the priestess Pythia, who was housed in the Temple of Apollo at Delphi (opposite).

To ensure the support of the immortals for any venture, ancient Greeks also worshipped them in elaborate ceremonies and appeased them with sacrifices. These rituals were often performed in magnificent temples dedicated to specific deities, such as the Parthenon of the goddess Athena in Athens, but were frequently only the focus during city-wide or national festivals that were milestones in the Greek calendar. As well as this very public display of reverence to the gods of Olympus, there were also a number of mystery cults devoted to some of the darker or more hedonistic deities of the pantheon, such as Hades and Dionysus, with exclusive membership and secret rites.

The Greek underworld

Having overthrown the Titans, the Olympian Gods divided the spoils. Zeus gained the kingdom of the air, his brother Poseidon, the kingdom of the sea and the eldest brother, Hades, the kingdom of the underworld. This subterranean realm, also known as Hades, was the destination of all mortals when they died.

It was customary to bury the dead with a coin on each eye and one under the tongue as fare for Charon (opposite), who ferried them across the rivers Styx and Acheron to Hades. Once through the gates, the dead were taken to one of five realms. Enemies of the gods were condemned to eternal torture in Tartarus, while criminals and sinners were consigned to the Fields of Punishment. Those who had led blameless but ordinary lives found an eternal resting place in the Meadows of Asphodel. The Elysian Fields were reserved for the most virtuous and heroic dead, who could choose either to stay or be reborn; if they returned to Elysium after three deserving lives, they would be sent to the most blissful of all afterlives in the Isles of the Blessed.

Roman mythology

The Roman civilization that developed in the first millennium BCE adopted elements of their religion from an earlier Italian people, the Etruscans. But as Roman influence in the Mediterranean grew, they more obviously appropriated much of the Greek pantheon, often simply giving the Greek gods Latin names and more recognizably Roman characteristics.

Zeus, for example, became Jupiter, his brothers Poseidon and Hades were identified with Neptune and Pluto, and Aphrodite was assigned the form of Venus. Dionysus, associated with an orgiastic mystery cult in Greece, took on a similar role in the form of the Roman Bacchus, who gave his name to the scandalous festivals of Bacchanalia. Much of the ancient Greek mythology dealing with the exploits and relationships of the gods was adapted to give it relevance to Roman society and customs, but also mingled with authentically Roman myths and history, such as the legend of Romulus and Remus and the foundation of Rome.

Major figures of the Graeco-Roman pantheon

GREEK	ROMAN	ROLE
Aphrodite	Venus	Goddess of love, beauty, fertility
Apollo	Apollo	God of music, prophecy, healing
Ares	Mars	God of war
Artemis	Diana	Goddess of hunting, the Moon
Athena	Minerva	Goddess of wisdom, war
Demeter	Ceres	Goddess of the harvest
Dionysus	Bacchus	God of wine and festivity
Eros	Cupid	God of love and sexual desire
Hades	Pluto	King of the Underworld
Hephaestus	Vulcan	God of fire and forges
Hera	Juno	Queen of the Gods
Hermes	Mercury	Messenger of the Gods
Hestia	Vesta	Goddess of the hearth
Pan	Pan	God of nature
Persephone	Proserpine	Queen of the Underworld
Poseidon	Neptune	God of the sea
Zeus	Jupiter	King of the Gods

Public and private Rome

The Romans considered religious ceremonies, sacrifices and festivals an important part of everyday life, essential in ensuring the favour of the gods. Religious ritual was so much a part of public life that religion and politics were inseparable, and the priests of the temples to various gods held positions in government. Politicians, military leaders and members of the royal family were expected to play a leading role in religious rites. The association of public figures with the gods was such that some emperors – for example, Augustus – were deified after death.

Not all religion was connected to the state, however, and numerous private cults existed, such as the Persian-rooted mystery cult of Mithraism popular among the military. The ordinary citizens of Rome also practised their own private religion, offering their devotion to spirits more relevant to their lives. These included Vesta, the goddess of the hearth and home, the Penates, the spirit guardians of the domestic larder, and the Lares, the spirits of the farmland and ancestral burial grounds.

The Vestal Virgins were custodians of one of Rome's most important temples.

Norse gods

The beliefs of the northern Germanic people are preserved in the rich tradition of Norse mythology, passed down orally for many generations and recorded in written form in Iceland in the 13th century. The Old Norse texts describe a sophisticated hierarchy of gods, giants and other mythical creatures.

The most respected deities are the Æsir, whose chief is the god Odin (opposite). With him are his wife, Frigg, goddess of wisdom and prediction, and their sons Höðr and Baldr. Other members of the Æsir include the hammer-wielding Thor and Týr, the god of war. Lesser gods, known as the Vanir, were defeated in battle by the Æsir and, later, the two combined to form a single pantheon. Among them are Njördr, the chief of the Vanir, and his children Freyr, god of fertility, and Freyja, a beautiful sorceress associated with love and war. Beneath the gods there is a race of giants, the Jötnar, led by Loki, whose many children include Hel, overseer of the underworld, the wolf-monster Fenrir and the serpent-monster Jörmungandr.

Norse cosmology

In Norse cosmology, the Universe has, at its centre, a massive ash tree, Yggdrasil, whose trunk links nine 'homeworlds' inhabited by all manner of humans, animals, gods and other mythical creatures.

Here, Asgard is the realm of the Æsir (the gods) and Midgard the home of humans. In others live the Vanir, the Jötnar, and the Dökkálfar and Ljósálfar, the dark and light dwarves. Yggdrasil's roots reach down into the underworld and the realms of Niflheim (homeworld of icy mist), Muspelheim (homeworld of fire) and the dark homeworld of Helheim.

Humans may spend the afterlife in any one of several worlds. Those who die valiantly in battle are taken by the Valkyries to Asgard, where they feast with Odin in Valhalla or rest in Freyja's meadow Fólkvangr. Others who died a natural death are sent to the care of the goddess Hel in Helheim. Those who led dishonourable lives are consigned to the icy wastes of Niflheim.

Ragnarök

The climax of Norse mythology is the battle at the end of the world, Ragnarök, which is fought between the Æsir (gods) and the Jötnar (giants). The word Ragnarök can be translated as 'fate of the gods' or 'twilight of the gods', which gives a clue as to its eventual outcome.

Odin, who leads the Æsir into war, is eaten by the wolf-monster Fenrir, who in turn is slain by Víðarr, Odin's son. Freyr and Thor are also both killed. While few of the Norse gods survive the battle, most of the goddesses remain untouched by the war. Led by Loki, the Jötnar and other monsters suffer similar losses, but despite being mortally wounded, Loki lives long enough to oversee the complete destruction of the Universe. From the ruins left by this apocalyptic conflict, a new and better world will emerge, heralding the beginning of a new era. Although not explicit in the various accounts of Ragnarök that exist, there is a suggestion in the myth that the Norse religion conceived of time as an eternal and cyclical process.

Mesoamerican religions

In the New World, civilizations arose as early as 1000 BCE, as people settled in the fertile areas of present-day Mexico. A distinctive Mesoamerican culture emerged, with a social structure underpinned by beliefs common to successive societies from the Olmecs and early Mayans in the first millennium BCE, through the Teotihuacan and Toltec people, to the Aztec Empire of the 14th to 16th centuries. Similar cultures, such as those of the Moche and Nazca and, subsequently, the Incas, later appeared in what is now Peru.

Religious belief revolved around rituals involving sacrifice of food, animals and even humans, overseen by a politically powerful class of priests. Ceremonies took place at specific times of the year, tying in with the agricultural cycle and astronomical events. The gods, and the temples dedicated to them, were associated with elements of a sophisticated calendrical system. The Aztecs, for example, linked the powerful gods of Wind and Rain, Quetzalcoatl and Tlaloc, with the complex motions of the planet Venus.

Mesoamerican temple complex
at Teotihuacan, Mexico

Zoroastrianism

The ancient Persian religion founded by the prophet Zoroaster in the late 2nd or early 1st millennium BCE is possibly the oldest faith to have continuously survived to the present day. Zoroastrianism is also often cited as the earliest known monotheistic religion, since Zoroaster chose the deity Ahura Mazda from the pantheon of traditional Persian and Indian religions as the supreme creator.

Ahura Mazda is the creator of seven lesser supernatural beings, the Amesha Spentas, but there also exists an evil spirit, Angra Mainyu. Conflict between Ahura Mazda and Angra Mainyu, the forces order and chaos, is at the core of Zoroastrian beliefs, and Zoroaster's teachings place great emphasis on human free will and responsibility for one's actions. By the sixth century BCE, Zoroastrianism had become the main religion of Persia, and remained a major world religion until it was superseded by Islam. Today, there are fewer than 200,000 followers, mostly living in India, where they are known as Parsis or Iranis.

Zoroastrian sacred site
at Yazd, Iran

Zoroaster

Little is known of the life of the founder of Zoroastrianism, except that he was an Avestan – one of the ethnic groups of ancient Persia, now present-day Iran and Afghanistan.

According to tradition, Zoroaster was born in the seventh century BCE, but it is now generally accepted that he lived much earlier, probably between 1700 and 1300 BCE. He was brought up in the polytheistic religion of the time, and from his teaching it is clear that he had some knowledge of the Indian religions that later became Hinduism. Legend has it that, aged 30, he had a vision that convinced him of the supremacy of one good creator, and from then spent his life preaching. He wrote a number of hymns (the Gathas) which, along with later texts by his followers in the Avestan language, form the Zoroastrian holy book, the Avesta. Zoroastrianism became the official religion of the Avestan people, but remained a minority faith until the unification of the Persian and Median Empires in the sixth century CE, when it spread across the whole of Persia.

Angels and demons

Although monotheistic in its reverence of Ahura Mazda, the unique creative spirit of the Universe, there is a dualism at the heart of Zoroastrian thought. The spiritual struggle of good against evil is symbolized by the opposing forces of Ahura Mazda and Angra Mainyu, and is reflected in the religion's Creation myth.

Zoroaster explained that Ahura Mazda has always existed, and has for all time been in conflict with Angra Mainyu. Both are transcendent spirits, responsible for the forces of order and chaos respectively. Before Ahura Mazda created the Universe, and then peopled it with humans, he emanated the spirit of Spenta Mainyu, or 'Good Spirit', and six other heavenly beings. Through these seven spirits, the Amesha Spentas, humans can understand the creator and use their free will to combat evil. He also created the *yazatas*, analogous to angels, to aid them in their fight. In response, Angra Mainyu, who does not have the power of creation, found ways to corrupt Ahura Mazda's creations, resulting in poisonous and pestilent creatures sent to plague humankind.

The winged disc of the Faravahar, representing a guardian angel, is an important symbol in both Zoroastrianism and secular Iranian identity.

Jainism

Jainism takes its name from the word *jina*, which literally means 'conqueror'. Here the word is used in a metaphorical and spiritual sense to mean 'enlightened teacher', and it is these *jinas* that Jains revere, rather than any deities.

According to Jain scriptures, Jainism can be traced back as far as the ninth century BCE, and the religion as it is known today was established in the sixth century BCE by the *jina* Mahavira. Jains believe, however, that Mahavira was simply the most recent of a line of 24 *jinas* of our present cosmic era, which stretches back countless billions of years. Like other Indian dharmic religions, Jainism holds that there is a cycle of death and rebirth, and that this can be escaped by contemplation and imitation of the example of the *jinas*. The Jain path to enlightenment is largely centred on the principles of personal responsibility and self-denial, and followers often lead lives of extreme asceticism. Today, Jainism has an estimated four to five million adherents, most of whom live in India.

Symbol representing the Jain principle of *ahimsa*, or nonviolence

The jinas

Jainism in its present form was founded by Prince Vardhamana (6th century BCE), who adopted the name Mahavira when he became a *jina* (spiritual teacher). A contemporary of Buddha (see page 130), Mahavira gave up his privileged life to seek enlightenment, and attained the status of *arihant* – one who has conquered all inner passions and attachments.

Mahavira devoted his life to teaching, becoming a *tirthankara*, to guide others towards liberation from the endless cycle of rebirth. Mahavira was the 24th of the *tirthankaras* or *jinas* recognized by Jainism as supreme beings, and was preceded by a ninth-century BCE teacher named Parshvanatha and, before him, a line of legendary and mythical spiritual leaders starting with Rishabhanatha. Within Jainism, there are five kinds of 'supreme being': *arhats*, those whose souls have been awakened, among whom are the *jinas*; *siddhas* (liberated souls); *acharyas* (leaders of the Jain religious order); *upadhyaya* (teachers of Jain monks and nuns); and *muni*, the monks and nuns.

Idol of Mahavir at the Jain pilgrimage site of Shri Mahavirji in Rajasthan

The Five Great Vows

Jains believe that liberation of the soul from the cycle of rebirth can be attained by following the example of the lives of the *tirthankaras* as a guide to progress through 14 steps to spiritual enlightenment. The wisdom of the *tirthankaras* is held in five basic principles, known as the Five Great Vows.

The first vow is *ahimsa*, nonviolence, which includes not causing injury of any kind to any living creature. Next is *satya*, telling the truth or, where this may cause injury, remaining silent. *Asteya* is the principle of not taking what is not freely offered (not only not stealing, but also forbidding extortion or cheating). The vow of *brahmacharya* is one of celibacy for monks and nuns; for the lay person it means chastity. Similarly, the vow of *aparigraha*, non-possessiveness, implies a rejection of attachment to materialism for the lay Jain, but an absolute renunciation of any form of ownership for the Jain monk or nun. While monastic orders adhere strictly to these vows, lay Jains are only asked to do their best to live their lives according to these principles.

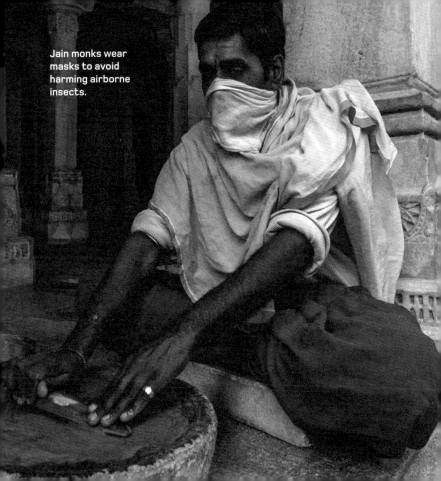

Jain monks wear masks to avoid harming airborne insects.

Jain worship

Because Jains believe that the Universe is eternal, without beginning or end, they reject the concept of a creator god. So, there is no place for worship as such in their religion, but instead a veneration of the 'supreme beings', and in particular meditation on the lives and teachings of the *jinas*. This usually takes the form of a daily ritual of contemplative devotion lasting for 48 minutes (one 30th of a day), which may be performed in a Jain temple or at a shrine in the home.

During meditation, Jains may focus their thoughts by *darshan* – that is, contemplating images of the *tirthankaras* and making eye contact with them – and may recite mantras such as the Namokar or Panca Namaskara paying homage to the five supreme beings (see page 74). Jains also celebrate their faith in a number of annual festivals, including the eight- or ten-day Paryushana. The final day of this event is the highpoint of the Jain calendar, Samvatsari, the Universal Day of Forgiveness, a time of confession of shortcomings and a renewal of vows.

18th-century devotional painting of humans and animals
gathering to hear the teachings of a *tirthankara*

Hinduism

Regarded as the world's third largest religion, Hinduism is in fact a coalition of many different religions with common roots in Indian tradition. It is only since the 19th century that the word 'Hinduism' has been adopted as an umbrella term for these Indian faiths.

Hinduism has no central authority, no single mythology, no standard rituals and a diversity of deities. The main unifying characteristic, however, is the distinctily Indian philosophical concept of dharma (see page 90) – the natural laws that govern order in the Universe and human behaviour, as described in ancient Sanskrit texts – and a belief in *samsara*, the cycle of death and rebirth. These beliefs can be traced back to ancient Indian religions as early as 1700 BCE, making Hinduism one of the oldest continuously surviving belief systems. Hinduism today is still mainly associated with India, where about 80 per cent of the population identify as Hindu, but also has large followings in Bangladesh and on the Indonesian island of Bali.

Vedic religion

The religions of India, collectively known as Hinduism, have origins in the Vedic culture that flourished between 1500 and 500 BCE. Religion at this time had a strong emphasis on ritual, involving a sacrificial fire and chanting of mantras to the gods, and a comprehensive mythology and cosmology.

Alongside numerous gods associated with natural phenomena, Vedic religion also included more abstract concepts of the forces at work in the cosmos. Chief among these were *satya* (truth) – the absolute quality of the oneness of the Universe – and *rta* (order or rule), the expression of *satya* in the natural order of the world. In Hinduism these concepts evolved into those of dharma and karma (see pages 90 and 96) and formed the basis for a system of ethics – how one should live in order to be in harmony with the cosmic laws. The Vedic people believed in the transmigration of the soul to another body after death, and following the principles of *satya* and *rta* would avoid punishment and ensure a successful rebirth.

Indra, god of thunder, lightning and rivers, is an important figure across all Vedic religions.

The Vedas

Hinduism is not founded on divine revelation or the message of a prophet, and so has no holy scriptures as such. Instead, the various traditions of Hinduism are derived from Sanskrit texts, known as the Vedas, which describe the customs and beliefs of the early Indian Vedic civilization.

Part of a much longer oral tradition, these texts are believed to have been first written down between 1200 and 900 BCE. Along with later texts including the Samhitas, Brahmanas and Upanishads, the Vedas are considered to be eternal truths recorded by sages. Collectively known as *shruti*, 'that which is heard', the texts contain instructions and commentaries on the rituals of Vedic religion. In the Upanishads, there is a detailed exploration of the philosophical and spiritual basis of the religion. Other texts, known as the *smriti* (that which is remembered), and which include the great epic poems *Ramayana* and *Mahabharata*, reiterate the beliefs and philosophy of the *shruti*, but do not have the same authority.

The god Brahma is depicted with four mouths, each of which is said to have produced one of the Vedas.

The cycle of rebirth

A central belief of all Vedic religions is the *atman*, the concept of an immortal soul. Everything in the Universe consists of two entities. The first is its own physical form, which can change and cease to exist; the second is its *atman* – its indestructible soul, spirit or essence.

Each of us is made up of physical matter, but we also have an *atman*, which is a part of the eternal, unchanging reality of the cosmos. Our bodies are born, they change and they die. After death, however, the *atman* is reborn in another body. This is not so much the reincarnation of a previous person as the transmigration of the spirit from one physical body to another, a journey of the soul known in Hinduism as *samsara*. In a constant cycle of birth, life, death and rebirth, the soul may take on countless different physical forms, each one determined by the conduct of the previous life or lives. Hindus believe that escape from the relentless cycle of *samsara* is possible, by following the correct way of life as described in the *shruti* texts (see page 84).

Great Wheel of Rebirth at the Buddhist site of Baodingshan, China

The four purusharthas

Hinduism has a huge number of deities within a wealth of mythology, but perhaps more important is the underlying philosophy that links them all. This concerns leading our lives in order to improve our own situation and that of those around us, while improving our chances of a good rebirth, or even an escape from perpetual *samsara* (see page 86).

For the Hindu, there are four *purusharthas* (objectives) in human life. The first of these is dharma meaning, in this context, the appropriate way to behave, and more generally the natural laws creating order in the world. A more practical everyday objective is *artha* (livelihood), which defines the morality of our economic values, our attitudes to work and wealth. Hinduism also recognizes that we have physical and emotional needs, which are categorized as *kama* (desire or sensual pleasure) and the appropriate ways to satisfy this. The final object of human pursuits is *moksha* (liberation), which refers to the ultimate goal of escape from *samsara*, as well as freedom from ignorance in this world.

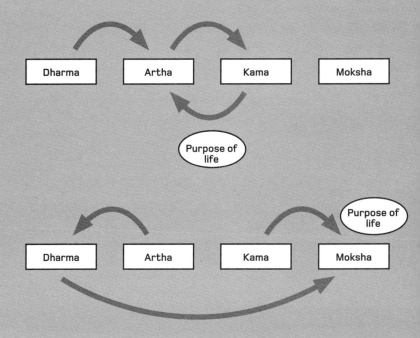

The worldly person becomes trapped in a cycle between artha and kama (top), unable to achieve moksha. The enlightened spirit, in contrast, disposes of wealth built up through artha according to dharma, which itself allows the achievement of moksha (bottom).

Dharma

In its widest sense, dharma describes the underlying laws that prevent the Universe from descending into chaos. There is an order to all things, and this is achieved by following the way laid out by dharma. In terms of human affairs, this is understood as the appropriate way to live in harmony with the natural order. It implies a code of ethics or moral values and the various duties and responsibilities placed on each one of us.

Dharma also implies virtue – living by the values of goodness and truth – and certain religious duties. Dharma is an obligation to live according to one's true nature and abilities, and so may vary from individual to individual; it is a teacher's dharma to instruct others, for example, and a father's dharma to protect and provide for his family. By following the path of their dharma, people contribute to the community and social order, which in turn plays a part in the balance of a Universe in which all things are interconnected, but also ensure progress in their souls' journey through *samsara* (see page 86).

The concept of dharma is often
represented by a spoked wheel,
the *dharmachakra*.

Artha and Kama

The ethical code implicit in the *purusharthas* (see page 88) extends beyond the purely theoretical morality of dharma to include practical guidelines for everyday life.

One of the most important objectives for most people is earning a living. This is encapsulated in the Hindu concept of *artha*, which suggests that in striving for prosperity one must work according to the principles of dharma (the natural order), and be aware of one's positive and negative effects in the world. By extension *artha* refers to economic values in general. These include attitudes to wealth and work, and even to commerce and governmental control of economic affairs.

A less tangible objective in life is the satisfaction of our emotional, sensual and aesthetic needs. Often misinterpreted by non-Hindus as being concerned only with sexual or romantic desires, *kama* in fact encompasses all these needs, regarding them as natural and healthy pursuits.

Erotic sculpture from Kandariya Mahadev Hindu Temple at Khajuraho

Moksha

Of the four *purusharthas* (see page 88), the most spiritually important is *moksha*, meaning liberation, and especially liberation from the cycle of death and rebirth.

There are several different interpretations of *moksha*, but it is generally thought of as a state of perfection beyond the material world, and a realization of the oneness of the *atman* or soul with the Universe. To attain the ultimate goal of *moksha*, an individual must live an appropriately virtuous life according to the dictates of dharma, *artha* and *kama* (see pages 90 and 92), but should also follow the *marga*, 'the way'.

There are three elements to *marga*: *kama-marga* (the way of appropriate conduct and actions); *jnana-marga* (the way of knowledge and insight, such as the practice of meditation and yoga); and *bhakti-marga* (the way of devotion to God). *Moksha* has the sense of realizing one's true potential through the knowledge gained by following the various paths of *marga*.

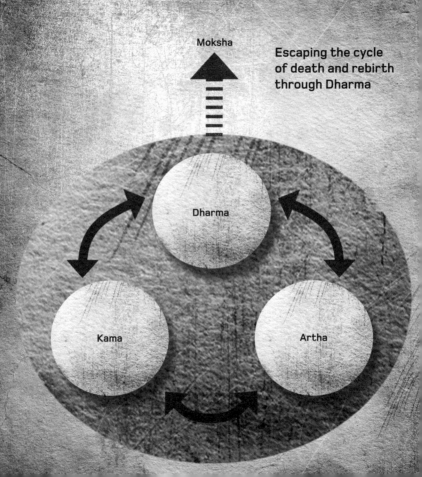

Karma

Hindus judge what is correct or appropriate according to the fundamental principle of cause and effect in the Universe, known as karma. Unlike the physical laws of cause and effect, however, karma is concerned with the spiritual effect that a person's actions and intentions have on themselves, rather than on others or the world around them.

Good deeds, and the right intentions, bring about good karma, which affects the individual's happiness in the future, while evil or inappropriate deeds and intentions attract bad karma and future suffering. Actions that are unintentional, whether good or bad, will not affect one's karma, neither is karma either the reward or punishment itself, but merely the underlying law that good fosters good, and evil fosters evil. The positive and negative effects of karma can be on a person's material, physical, emotional or moral wellbeing, bringing about happiness or suffering in their current life. It can also affect the *atman* as it goes through the cycle of *samsara*.

What you do...

...affects you in this life...

...and the next.

Karma

Ahimsa

From the concept that each individual's soul or *atman* is ultimately an integral part of an interconnected Universe, Hinduism places great value on respect for all living things. Because of this, one of the most valued virtues is the practice of *ahimsa* (nonviolence).

As well as renouncing any violence towards other humans, many Hindus are also vegetarian or vegan and almost all avoid eating beef (the cow, although not 'sacred', is valued for providing milk and natural fertilizer so has an honoured place in Indian culture). Even those who do eat meat advocate the *jhatka* method of killing animals quickly and painlessly, rather than ritual slaughter. Hinduism does however recognize that there are situations in which *ahimsa* is not the appropriate course of action, and would therefore not be in accord with dharma (see page 90). For example, in the Bhagavadgita, a central section of the epic *Mahabharata*, the hero Arjuna is reluctant to go into battle, but is persuaded by Krishna that it is his duty.

Mohandes K Gandhi rooted his influential campaign for Indian independence from Britain on the principle of *ahimsa*.

Four stages of life

A person following his or her dharma (see page 90) can expect to go through several different stages in life. Hinduism recognizes four of these, the *ashramas*, as linking the different periods of our Earthly lives with steps in our spiritual development.

The first stage is *brahmacharya*, a period of learning that corresponds to the life of a young student whose time is most usefully spent developing physical and mental capabilities, but also developing spiritually by studying the scriptures and learning from a guru. This is followed by *grihastha*, life as a householder – marrying, raising a family and working – but also doing things that benefit others and society in general. *Vanaprastha* is a period of withdrawal, marked by retirement from work and with the family grown up, when an individual can take time to contemplate and meditate. Few people embark upon the final stage, *sannyasa*, characterized by detachment from the material world and leading life as an ascetic.

Adi Shankara (8th century CE) was an influential teacher who pursued *sannyasa* from an early age, and unified many of the principles of Hindu philosophy.

Social classes

According to the Vedic tradition, society is composed of *varnas* (social classes), which correspond to the various attributes of Purusha, the prototypical cosmic man. The *varnas* are determined by vocation rather than birth, and each has a respected place in society as a whole. Hinduism identifies four of these social divisions: Brahmins (priests and teachers); Kshatriyas (rulers and warriors); Vaishyas (traders and farmers); and Shudras (workers and servants).

The *varnas* may have influenced the formation of the Indian castes, but the two should not be confused. The caste system is a social, rather than religious classification, based on a hierarchy from ruling class down to 'untouchables', and divided by hereditary associations of certain families or communities with particular occupations. In contrast, the *varnas* are classified according to an individual's dharma (see page 90). It is a less discriminatory system, therefore, with mutual respect between *varnas*, and only the Brahmins regarded as a superior class.

Brahmins
(priests)

Kshatriyas
(warriors)

Vaishyas
(merchants and landowners)

Shudras
(Workers and servants)

Untouchables
(Grievous sinners and
barbarians)

'Twice-born'
groups that
go through a
later spiritual
initiation

Brahma and the
Hindu pantheon

As a coalition of many different religious traditions, Hinduism has a bewildering array of gods and goddesses. There is, however, a general consensus among branches of Hinduism as to the existence of a supreme creator god, Brahma. Along with Vishnu the preserver god and Shiva the destroyer god, Brahma forms a trinity known as the Trimurti. These three principal gods are the embodiment of aspects of *atman* (see page 86) and correspond to stages in the cycles of the cosmos – creation, preservation and destruction.

There are numerous lesser deities, each with their own following in different branches of Hinduism. Many of these gods take on different forms and are known by different names, or manifest themselves as avatars. With so many gods and goddesses, Hinduism is generally seen as an obviously polytheistic religion, but there is a prevalent belief in a single supreme being, and the Trimurti as three aspects of that one being, accompanied by a pantheon of minor deities.

The Trimurti, with associated minor deities and key incarnations

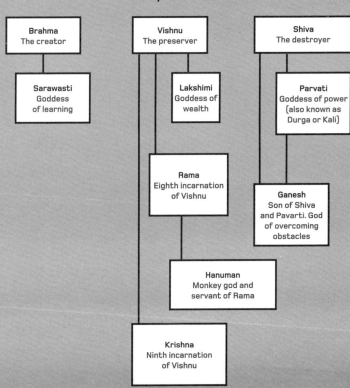

Vishnu

Of the gods of the Trimurti, Brahma is the supreme creator. With his work of creation complete, he is rarely prayed to in the same way as Vishnu and Shiva, whose influences in the world are still active. Vishnu is characterized as the preserver and protector of the cosmos. Regarded as the embodiment of the Universe itself, he is generally depicted as a blue-skinned being, with four arms representing the four points of the compass. Often each hand holds a symbol of his power: a mace for control and order; a conch shell, the sound of which represents the origin of the Universe; a disc, representing the dominion over which he is lord; and a lotus, symbol of purity and fertility. Vishnu is known as a god who takes many forms, and manifests himself on Earth as one of ten avatars. To date he has appeared as Matsya (the fish), Kurma (the turtle), Varaha (the boar), Narasimha (half lion, half man), Vamana (the dwarf), Parashurama (the Brahmin), and most famously as the warrior Rama, the heroic Prince Krishna, and the Buddha. Kalki is an incarnation yet to come.

Shiva

The third deity of the Trimurti, Shiva, is known as the destroyer, but more accurately can be regarded as the god balancing the opposing forces of destruction and creation, and representing the cyclical nature of the Universe. He has a dual role – at times benevolent, at others fierce – and he is depicted as both destroyer and saviour, removing evil and clearing the ground for change and renewal. Like Brahma and Vishnu, he is an aspect of universal reality, *brahman*, and is worshipped as the highest god by the Shaivite branch of Hinduism (see page 124).

More popularly, he is depicted as the Lord of the Dance, surrounded by a circle of fire, the symbol of his destructive power, and stamping on a demon to the beat of his drum. Rather than manifesting himself as avatars, as Vishnu does, Shiva expresses the different facets of his character through his many consorts, who include the goddesses Durga, Kali and Parvati (see page 112).

Ganesh

Although a minor deity in comparison to the gods of the Trimurti (see page 104), the elephant-headed god Ganesh is one of the most popular Hindu gods, worshipped throughout India as the remover of obstacles and bringer of good fortune.

There are several legends explaining his distinctive elephant's head. The most common of these is that, while protecting his mother Parvati, he was beheaded by his father Shiva, who did not recognize him. Shiva then vowed to replace the head with that of the first creature he saw, which happened to be an elephant. As well as his characteristic benevolence, Ganesh is generally associated with wisdom and learning, and is traditionally believed to be the first scribe, breaking off one of his tusks to use as a pen in order to write down the epic poem *Mahabharata*, dictated to him by the sage Vyasa. He is generally depicted as pot-bellied, and holding a bowl of sweetmeats, leading to the custom of leaving these as an offering at shrines devoted to him.

Hindu goddesses

While the gods of the Trimurti are male, Hinduism recognizes that there is also a feminine divine force, Shakti, which is embodied in the numerous Hindu goddesses. Chief of these is Maha Devi, the Great Mother Goddess, who personifies the creative power of *brahman*.

There are also many lesser goddesses, representing various female aspects of the Universe, such as fertility, nurturing, creativity and beauty, as well as some more destructive powers. Many goddesses are consorts of the gods, and are regarded as complementary to them. These include the river deity Saraswati, wife of the creator god Brahma. She is the personification of the life-giving principle and goddess of wisdom and knowledge. Vishnu's consort Lakshmi complements his role as preserver and is goddess of material and spiritual good fortune. The many consorts of Shiva include Parvati, the gentle goddess of love and devotion, but also the fierce warrior goddess Durga, and the violent and terrible Kali, goddess of time, destruction and death.

Kali dances on the prone form of her consort Shiva.

Hindu worship

Comprising a number of different religious traditions, Hinduism has no standard form of worship, and the practice of devotional rituals is largely a matter of regional, or even personal, choice. Temples are often the focus of communal celebrations during festivals and to mark rites of passage, such as weddings and funerals, where ceremonies such as the fire ritual *yajna* are performed.

However, many Hindus prefer to perform their devotions at home. These are performed at small domestic shrines that are decorated with images of the worshippers' preferred deities. There is no set order to follow for these rituals. Usually, lamps and incense are lit, and prayers and offerings are made to one or more of the gods, accompanied by singing or chanting of Vedic hymns and readings from the Hindu texts. Many Hindus worship on a regular basis – sometimes weekly, and typically on a Thursday – while the more devout will worship daily at dawn and also spend time devoted to quiet meditation.

Hindu temples

While many Hindus choose to worship at a domestic shrine in the home, the temple is still an important centre of the Hindu community, especially for occasions such as festivals and as a destination for pilgrimages. Hindu temples range from simple village halls to elaborately decorated complexes of buildings, and are built in a wide range of architectural styles.

In southern India, many have a large gateway topped with an ornate monumental tower, while in the north, temples are more rounded in shape. In all, however, the building follows the same basic plan. There is a central inner sanctum and shrine, the *garbhagriha*, which houses an icon of the deity, and is surrounded by an area around which worshippers can walk. There may also be a congregation hall and various other rooms for dancing or ritual offerings. The architecture of the temple is rich in symbolism, as it is not only the home of the god to whom it is dedicated, but also represents various aspects of the human body and the cosmology of the Universe.

Nandalal temple in Bishnupur in the Indian state of West Bengal

Hindu festivals

With so many gods and goddesses, Hinduism provides the opportunity for a large number of celebrations. The Hindu calendar is full of festivals, some of which are observed by all Hindus, and others by followers of a particular deity or in a specific region. During festivals, which may last several days, the distinctions of social class are largely overlooked, and people join together in worship, feasting and celebration.

The most important universally observed festivals are Holi, the celebration of spring and the New Year; Dussera, commemorating Rama's victory over evil; and Diwali, the festival of lights in honour of Vishnu. Many Hindus also show their devotion by pilgrimage to a holy site. These sites usually mark a significant legendary event or the place in which a deity is believed to reside. They can be prominent places such as the mountains of the Himalayas or cities. Varanasi, the 'City of Light' on the banks of the river Ganges, for example, is revered by believers as a manifestation of the god Shiva.

Hindu fire ritual at Varanasi

Yoga and meditation

Meditation has been an important aspect of Hinduism since its beginnings in the Vedic times. As the religion evolved, so, too, did the combined physical and mental discipline of yoga.

The practice of yoga is described in the Upanishads in about 500 BCE, but the most respected book devoted to the subject is the *Yoga Sutras*, a collection of nearly 200 aphorisms, by the Hindu scholar Patanjali in about 400 CE. He describes yoga as a method of achieving a state of consciousness free from 'modifications of the mind', distracting thoughts, and awareness of anything external. The combination of physical and mental concentration helps to overcome the 'wrong' process of active thinking, in order to expand one's consciousness. In this way, the practitioner can become one with everything in the Universe, and gain spiritual insight into the illusory, impermanent nature of the material world, and the transcendent, permanent nature of reality. Yoga is practised by many Hindus as an aid to *marga*, the way to *moksha* (see page 94).

Sadhus and gurus

The emphasis in Hinduism is on personal devotion and worship carried out in the home, so there is no clergy as such. The Brahmins, the traditional class of priests (see page 102), may be called upon to lead some rituals, but more important in Hindu culture is the guru – teacher and scholar. The guru's primary role is to instruct, particularly young people in the first stage of their journey through life, *brahmacharya*. As well as teaching the content of the Hindu texts and interpretation of their meaning, gurus help students acquire the skills of meditation and yoga, and guide their spiritual development.

Another revered figure in the Hindu community is the sadhu, or holy man. Also known as a *swami* or *sanyasi* (the less common female sadhu is known as a *sanyasini*), a sadhu has entered the fourth stage of life, *sanyasa*, renouncing the material world and dedicating himself to spiritual contemplation and devotion. Some live communally as monks in a monastery, while others live a nomadic existence with no possessions, and survive by begging.

Branches of Hinduism

Hinduism is a description of the loose coalition of religions of India. There are many regional variations of both belief and practice, and branches devoted to one or more different deities of the enormous Hindu pantheon. Broadly speaking, however, there are four main traditions. They are not mutually exclusive and many followers belong to more than one denomination.

Vaishnavism emphasizes the primacy of Vishnu (see page 106). More than other Hindu sects, Vaishnavites practise communal worship in often ecstatic rituals, with the temple playing a dominant role. Shaivism similarly focuses on the worship of Shiva (see page 108). This is generally the most ascetic of the branches of Hinduism, and Shaivites tend to practise individual devotion rather than ritual. In Shaktism, the feminine principle, *shakti*, is worshipped in the form of Maha Devi, the mother goddess, and the other major goddesses. (see page 112). Smartism has no one primary god, but instead recognizes several deities as manifestations of *brahman*, the Absolute.

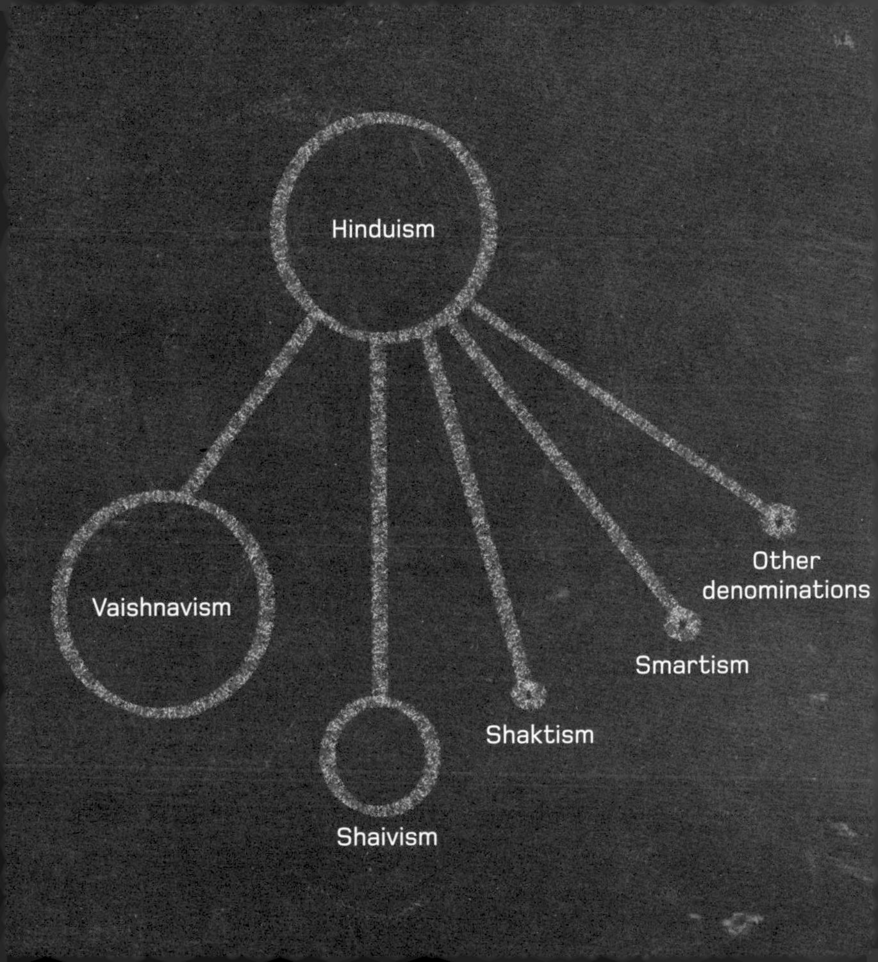
Hinduism
Vaishnavism
Shaivism
Shaktism
Smartism
Other denominations

Hare Krishna

Hinduism was largely overlooked in the West until the 19th century, when translations of the Vedic texts became available in Europe. Interest was also spurred by the revitalization of Hinduism by the mystic Sri Ramakrishna and his followers at the turn of the 20th century.

The pop culture of the 1960s introduced many in the West to Indian culture and religion, with celebrities such as the Beatles taking up transcendental meditation with the guru Maharishi Mahesh Yogi. In the wake of this, A. C. Bhaktivedanta Swami Prabhupada established a new religious movement, the International Society for Krishna Consciousness (ISKCON) in New York in 1966. A sect of Vaishnavism (see page 124), it advocates the practice of *bhakti* yoga, with the focus of love and devotion on Vishnu's avatar Krishna. It gained a popular following in the West, and in the 1960s and 1970s many adherents could be seen in their orange robes, dancing and chanting the mantra that earned them the nickname the 'Hare Krishnas'.

Buddhism

The sixth century BCE saw a flowering of intellectual activity in many civilizations around the world. In Greece, this produced the first philosophers; in China, the sages Laozi and Confucius (see pages 172 and 176); and in the north of India, Siddhartha Gautama – the Buddha – founded a religious tradition that broke away from the prevailing Vedic trends.

Buddhism shifted emphasis from the traditional worship of gods to individual spiritual development and understanding, advocating an approach to life that could bring liberation from suffering and the relentless cycle of death and rebirth. Through his insights and teachings, Buddha gained a small following during his lifetime, and his ideas rapidly spread from northern India across most of Asia, and eventually worldwide. Buddhism today is the world's fourth largest religion with an estimated 500 million followers – eight per cent of the world's population. In the last half century, however, for perhaps the first time since its foundation, numbers have seen a gradual decline.

The Buddha

Buddhism differs from most other religions in many respects: most strikingly, it makes no mention of deities or supernatural beings, and is based not on divine revelation or inspiration, but on the ideas of one man, Siddhartha Gautama, better known as 'the Buddha'. He assumed the title *buddha*, meaning 'enlightened one', after many years of exploring different meditative and ascetic religious disciplines led him to recognise a different path to spiritual fulfilment.

Gautama was not a divine being, a saint, nor even a prophet, but an inquisitive and thoughtful scholar, a philosopher who arrived at his insight into and understanding of the mysteries of life through experience, contemplation and rational thought. He is revered by his followers as a sage and teacher rather than the bringer of a divine message, and thus Buddhism has neither holy scriptures nor a mythology of its own. Instead, it is built upon the collected teachings and sayings of the Buddha, and commentaries on them by subsequent Buddhist scholars.

The life of
Siddhartha Gautama

There are many accounts of Gautama's life. What is not disputed, however, is that he was born in the Bihar region of northern India some time in the sixth or fifth century BCE and lived to about the age of 80. He was born into a relatively prosperous family, with the prospect of following his father as a leader of the community. As a student of religion, however, he found little satisfaction in his sheltered lifestyle, and was especially upset at the prevalence of suffering in the world.

He reacted by renouncing his privileged life, leaving his wife and family, and taking up a succession of harsh ascetic disciplines. These gave him no satisfaction either. It was when sitting in contemplation under a fig tree (the Bodhi tree, the 'tree of awakening') that he had the insight that formed the basis of his religious and philosophical thinking. After six years of meditation, he believed he had reached a state of enlightenment. He spent the rest of his life as a travelling teacher, and established a monastic order devoted to his ideas.

Mahabodhi temple complex in India's Bihar province marks the site where Gautama achieved enlightenment under the Bodhi tree.

The teachings of Buddha

The Buddha Gautama left no written record of his teachings; instead, they were passed down orally for centuries after his death. His ideas had spread across India by the time the first Buddhist scriptures were written, in the Pali language of Sri Lanka. The three volumes of the Pali canon, known as Tripitaka ('three baskets') are considered the most authoritative Buddhist texts, compiled in the first century from the teachings passed down orally by members of his monastic order.

The first, the Vinaya Pitaka, is a set of guidelines for the conduct of Buddhist monasteries; the second, the Sutta Pitaka, is a collection of sayings and lessons attributed to the Buddha. The final volume, the Abhidhamma Pitaka, comprises commentaries on the teachings, and there is no single standard version — the various traditions of Buddhism include texts that are most relevant to their interpretation of the Buddha's teaching. Many other texts have been added over the centuries, but they are not accepted as having the authority of the Tripitaka.

Indian roots

Siddhartha Gautama was born in India at a time when the religious traditions now known as Hinduism were beginning to emerge. He was brought up with the beliefs of the ancient Vedic religions, including the concepts of *samsara*, dharma and karma (see pages 80, 90 and 96). These concepts were deeply ingrained within Indian culture, and lie at the heart of the so-called dharmic religions of Hinduism and Jainism. But new religious movements during Gautama's lifetime challenged some of the assumptions of the Vedic religions, and in this sceptical atmosphere he was disinclined to accept things on faith alone. Instead, he placed a greater emphasis on meditation, another feature common to all the Indian religious traditions, through which the individual could attain enlightenment without any involvement with supernatural forces, such as *brahman* and the gods. As with the other dharmic religions, the goal is to escape the suffering of eternal birth and rebirth, but in Buddhism the ultimate aim is nirvana, 'not-being', rather than a state of perfection.

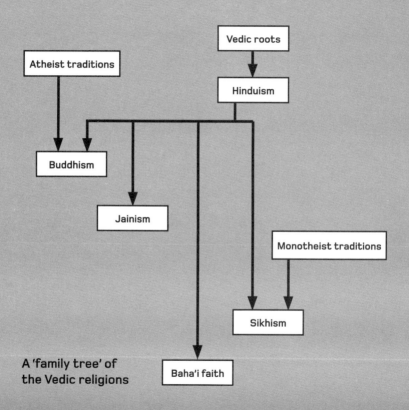

A 'family tree' of the Vedic religions

The Middle Way

In his quest for answers to the mysteries of life, Gautama moved from his previous life of material and sensual indulgence to that of a strict ascetic. But neither had given him the spiritual satisfaction he was looking for and he came to realize that there was another way to live. He described this as the Middle Way, avoiding the extremes of indulgence and self-mortification, of trying to satisfy our needs and desires all the time or trying to deny them by harsh austerity.

It was by adopting this path of moderation that he achieved the calm he needed to meditate and gain insight. But he also used the term to describe his understanding of the opposing religious ideas that were being proposed at the time. He felt that there was a middle way between the unquestioning belief of traditional religion and complete scepticism, and similarly a middle way between the ideas of eternal existence inherent in the Vedic religions and the permanent nonexistence suggested by materialist philosophers.

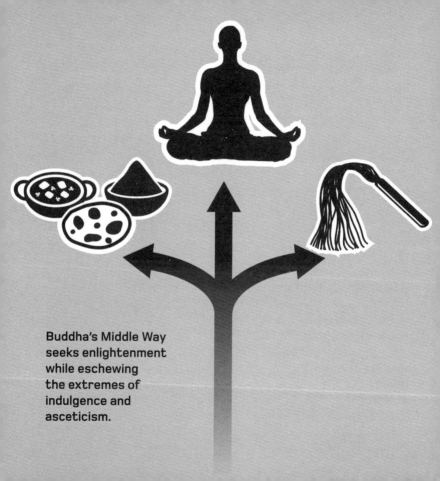

Buddha's Middle Way seeks enlightenment while eschewing the extremes of indulgence and asceticism.

The marks of existence

In contemplating the nature of our existence, the Buddha Gautama arrived at conclusions that were very different from the emerging Hindu beliefs. Most fundamentally, he rejected the traditional concept of an eternal and unchanging soul, the *atman* (see page 86).

There are, he said, three distinguishing features of our being, the three 'marks of existence': *anatta*, not-self; *anicca*, impermanence; and *dukkha*, suffering. To accept these marks of existence is to contradict the idea of *atman*. Buddha argued that everything that exists has come into being dependent on all other things that exist, that there is no independent 'self', but instead 'not-self'. Everything that exists is constantly subject to change. The interdependence of things for their very existence implies a chain of causes that results in death and rebirth, but rather than being the reincarnation of an eternal and unchanging soul, to the Buddhist it is one's consciousness that is reborn, and that ceases with liberation from *samsara*.

HINDUISM

BUDDHISM

Moksha

Nirvana

Escape from the cycle
of death and rebirth,
salvation for the
eternal soul

Liberation from death
and rebirth, and an
end to existence and
consciousness

Escape from reincarnation in Hinduism and Buddhism

The Four Noble Truths

According to legend, when the Buddha Gautama first left the protection of his comfortable home he was shocked by life outside. Observing an old man, a sick man, a dead man and an ascetic, he saw how much suffering there was in the world. It put his own dissatisfaction into perspective.

This realization became the cornerstone of what he later described as Four Noble Truths that a Buddhist must accept before embarking on the path to enlightenment. The first is *dukkha*, generally translated as 'suffering' but also meaning 'unsatisfactoriness'. The truth of *dukkha* is that it is always necessary as one of the marks of existence (see page 140). The second truth, *samudaya*, explains that *dukkha* results from our craving for impermanent things and attachment to illusory things that can never be satisfied. *Nirodha* says that there can be an end to *dukkha* if we bring an end to wanting and attachment to things. Finally, *marga*, explains that, in order to achieve this, we must follow the Eightfold Path (see page 144).

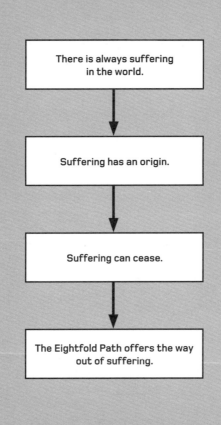

The Eightfold Path

The Buddha Gautama taught that there are eight different attitudes that must be adopted in overcoming the wants and attachments that cause suffering and so tie us to *samsara* (see page 80).

This Eightfold Path offered a checklist of ways to approach life, giving advice on spiritual development, living ethically, and focusing the mind. The first attitude – right view – involves accepting and understanding the Four Noble Truths. The second – right intention – demands a commitment to learning and growth. The next three – right speech, right action and right livelihood – concern behaviour in our everyday lives, and the importance of human morality.

Finally, the principles of right effort, right mindfulness and right concentration are instructions for practising meditation – correctly directing one's thoughts to see through the ephemeral world – and overcoming one's ego to reach enlightenment.

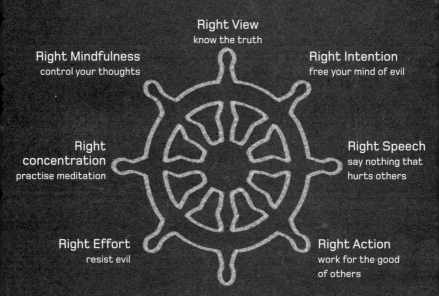

The Eightfold Path

Right View
know the truth

Right Mindfulness
control your thoughts

Right Intention
free your mind of evil

Right concentration
practise meditation

Right Speech
say nothing that hurts others

Right Effort
resist evil

Right Action
work for the good of others

Right Livelihood
respect life

Enlightenment

The word 'enlightenment' is used loosely as a translation of several different concepts in Buddhism. Its primary sense is as a translation of *bhodi*, the 'awakening' or 'understanding' that Gautama experienced when meditating under the fig tree.

This is often understood as a spontaneous insight. However, although Gautama no doubt had an 'aha' moment of realization, he is said to have spent 50 days in meditation under the Bodhi tree, and several more years of contemplation before attaining *bodhi*, the complete understanding that earned him Buddhahood. The sudden insight is only a part of *bodhi*, or awakening.

The word 'enlightenment' is also used in the West to describe, not only the process of understanding, but the end result. In this sense, the Buddha is said to have gained enlightenment – an awakening – from his insight and understanding. In some senses, enlightenment can also mean the state of liberation from the suffering of existence that comes with *bodhi*.

A statue of the Buddha sits beneath a Bodhi tree at a Buddhist shrine in Thailand

Nirvana

As with the other dharmic religions, Buddhism is based on a belief in a cycle of birth, death and rebirth, and its goal is freedom from this cycle. But the nature of this liberation in Buddhism is unlike that of other faiths. While we exist for life upon life, we experience *dukkha*, suffering and unsatisfactoriness. If we can achieve enlightenment, however, we have the opportunity to enter a state beyond existence and rebirth – nirvana.

The sanskrit word *nirvana* literally means 'extinguishing'. To the Buddhist it means an end to *samsara*, but also the cessation of suffering and dissatisfaction, a cessation of consciousness and a realization of the not-self. This is not the destination of an eternal soul, but the dispassionate peace of not-being – an escape from existence – and is characterized by what it is not and what has ceased to be. A person who has achieved *bodhi* (enlightenment) has reached a state of incomplete nirvana, in which he or she remains until death, when he/she makes the transition to complete or final nirvana.

The achievement of nirvana is often compared to the snuffing out of a candle in Buddhist traditions.

Buddhas and bodhisattvas

Siddhartha Gautama assumed the title Buddha (from the word *bodhi*) when he believed that he had fully understood the truths of existence, and the way to achieve liberation from it. According to some Buddhist traditions, he was not the first to have merited the title, but is revered as the Buddha whose teachings brought Buddhism to the world.

In the Mahayana tradition, Gautama Buddha's life as a teacher is emulated as well as revered. People following his example of sharing their knowledge and understanding of *bodhi* are known as *bodhisattvas* and are respected as sources of spiritual guidance. Like Gautama Buddha, they have achieved enlightenment, but delay their transition to final nirvana until their deaths, in order to help others reach the same stage of awakening. Often, these *bodhisattvas* come from monastic orders, or have otherwise devoted their lives to meditation to achieve *bodhi*, and have taken a vow to use their insight to bring about the enlightenment of the whole world.

This 6th-century Chinese mural shows worshipping bodhisattvas.

Buddhist meditation

A key distinguishing feature of Buddhism is that Gautama's ideas came from contemplation, and traditional images depict him seated cross-legged, with a peaceful smile on his face. Since this was the means by which he achieved his enlightenment, regular meditation is regarded as an essential practice for his followers.

Three elements of the Eightfold Path (see page 144) refer directly to the correct attitudes necessary for meditation. Buddha is said to have experimented with several methods himself, including extreme asceticism and harsh self-mortification, but without success. Instead, he sought a middle way between thoughtlessness and the strict disciplines followed by many holy men. In recollecting a childhood memory of sitting alone under a tree, he saw this as the ideal state of mind for meditation that would lead to 'awakening': free from thoughts of pleasure or pain, mindful and focused rather than distracted, and concentrating on the truths of being and not-being.

Monks and monasteries

There is a strong monastic tradition in most branches of Buddhism, stemming from the order of monks established by Buddha himself. Several orders exist, each with different rules and disciplines. In general, however, a young person enters an order as a *sramanera* (novice) and after a period of learning may become a *bhikkhu* (ordained monk) or *bhikkhuni* (nun).

The word *bhikkhu* means 'someone who lives on alms', and Buddhist monks take vows renouncing the material world to devote themselves to a life, not only of meditation, but also of service to the community in return for its charity. Monks in the Mahayana orders may also undertake to become *bodhisattvas* (see page 150) to help others reach enlightenment. Although in several orders boys as young as eight years old may join as *sramaneras*, it is generally not a lifetime commitment. Adult *bhikkhus*, although they promise to live an austere and celibate life, may retain contact with their families, and have the option to return to life outside the order when they want.

Temples and stupas

Buddhism mentions no deities and so worship does not play a part in Buddhist practices. Instead, the emphasis is on individual spiritual development through meditation. But that is not to say that Buddhism lacks a ritual element – in many traditions there are formal communal ceremonies performed in purpose-built temples.

Ceremonies range from simple rituals to provide conditions for meditation, to more elaborate services of devotion to the Buddha as a quasi-divine saviour. There are also more ecstatic gatherings to give an insight into what it is like to be enlightened. Temples exist in a wide variety of styles. Some are modest buildings, decorated with images of the Buddha or symbols associated with mantras (chants and sounds to aid meditation). Others are ornate temple complexes, lavishly decorated with images of the life of the Buddha and *bodhisattvas*. The many distinctive stupas across the Buddhist world – domed shrines housing the relics of *bodhisattvas* – serve as places of meditation.

Philosophy or religion?

Buddhism is more concerned with individual spirituality and morality than cosmology. The movement Gautama founded is based on ideas, thought and consciousness, and provides a practical framework for living a life that will bring spiritual satisfaction. Some would argue, therefore, that it is not really a religion, as it involves no deities, worship or divine revelation, but simply a philosophy – a rational way of explaining the world, and practical guidelines of morality. But this ignores the fact that there are certain aspects of Buddhism that rely on faith.

For example, much of the reasoning in Buddhism is based on the assumption that there is such a thing as *samsara* (see page 80), and that this is affected by the cosmic laws of dharma and karma. These are matters of faith, rather than rational argument. Buddhism could be regarded as a form of philosophy incorporating elements of the supernatural, or described as a nontheistic religion. Or, perhaps as Gautama himself might have put it, a middle way between religion and philosophy.

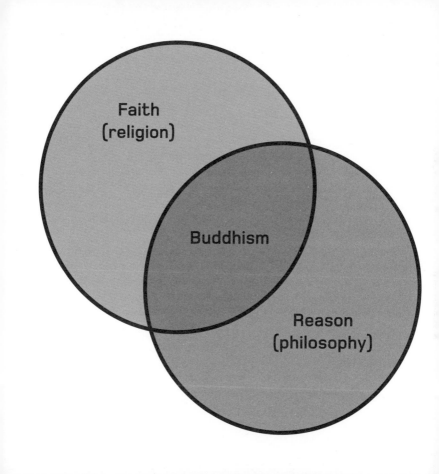

The spread of Buddhism

Following his enlightenment, Buddha devoted his life to teaching others. He travelled around northern India and Nepal and gained a small following of disciples. Gradually, his ideas spread southwards into the rest of India.

The religion had reached as far south as Sri Lanka by the time of the Greek colonization of northern India, which helped to spread the religion westwards from around 180 BCE. It also spread to cities on Asian trade routes that carried Buddhism across the Himalayas into China. Sea-going trade from Sri Lanka, meanwhile, took it into Thailand and other parts of South-east Asia.

Buddhism declined in India under the Muslim Mogul Empire (16th–19th centuries), and more recently has been suppressed by communist regimes or threatened by conservative Islamic states, yet in many countries including China it remains the dominant religion. Despite its status in Asia, Buddhism has only recently acquired a significant following in Europe and America.

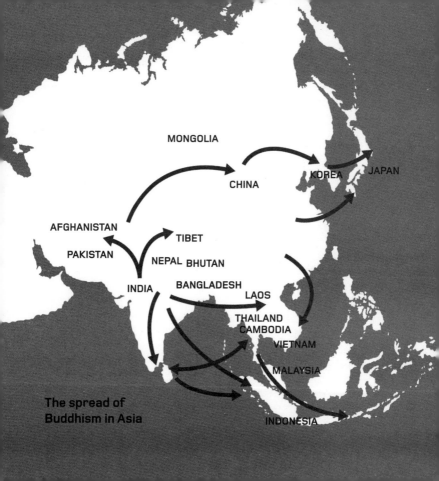

The spread of
Buddhism in Asia

Theravada Buddhism

The oldest branch of Buddhism, and probably closest to the original tradition, is Theravada, meaning the 'School of the Elders'. It evolved from the earliest traditions of Buddhism that spread across India, and which survived mainly in the south of the subcontinent and Sri Lanka. It was here that the Pali canon was compiled, which forms the core doctrine of the Theravada tradition. The tradition travelled to South-east Asia, and became the predominant form of Buddhism in Thailand, Laos, Cambodia and Myanmar (formerly Burma).

Compared with other Buddhist denominations, it is somewhat conservative and sometimes austere, with an emphasis on individual meditation, discipline and rationalism, rather than ceremony, and a strong tradition of monasticism. Having said that, Theravada temples are often sumptuously decorated, and feature images of the Buddha depicted as a majestic figure. Today, about one-third of Buddhists are followers of Theravada Buddhism.

Giant reclining
Buddha at
Chauk Htat Gyi
Pagoda in Myanmar's
commercial
centre of Yangon

Mahayana Buddhism

The largest of the major branches of Buddhism, Mahayana (meaning 'Great Vehicle') accounts for more than half of all Buddhists and is the dominant form in China, Japan and Vietnam. It developed from the ideas expressed in the Mahayana Sutras – commentaries on the original Buddhist texts, thought to have been written some time around the beginning of the Common Era. These were especially influential as Buddhism spread through Tibet and China to Mongolia, as well as in their homeland of the Indian subcontinent.

A key difference between Mahayana and the older Theravada tradition is its focus on the *bodhisattva* (see page 150). Mahayana regards the Theravada emphasis on individual enlightenment as contrary to the spirit of Buddha's example, and so aspires, not to personal nirvana, but to Buddhahood, by which they can bring about universal liberation from *samsara*. The ceremonies of Mahayana tend to be more devotional and verge on a worship of Buddha as a semi-divine saviour.

The Mahayana Buddhist temple of Borobudur on the Indonesian island of Java

Vajrayana Buddhism

The third of the main Buddhist traditions, Vajrayana developed from a sect of Indian Buddhists in the eighth century, and today is practised mainly in the Himalayan countries of Tibet and Bhutan. It is sometimes referred to as Tantric Buddhism, as it incorporates techniques of meditation described in the esoteric Hindu texts known as the Tantras.

Over a period of centuries, Vajrayana (the 'Diamond Way') evolved to include the use of yoga, along with mantras and mandalas in elaborate rituals to aid meditation. Unlike Theravada meditation, where the ultimate aim is nirvana, or the Mahayana goal of becoming a *bodhisattva*, Vajrayana rituals are a way for followers to realize 'Buddha nature'. This is not the same as enlightenment or nirvana (see pages 130 and 148), nor even merely understanding the concept intellectually, but experiencing it emotionally and physically, too. Vajrayana is an oral tradition, passed from teacher to student, as this is knowledge believed to be impossible to learn from texts.

Masked performers in
a traditional Nepalese
Buddhist play

Zen Buddhism

As Buddhism gained followers in China, it was influenced by the philosophies of Daoism and Confucianism (see pages 174 and 176). The resulting school of thought, Chan Buddhism, was later adopted in Vietnam and Korea, and in Japan, where it became known as Zen Buddhism – the name most familiar in the West.

With roots in the Mahayana tradition (see page 164), Zen has an emphasis on order and discipline. It shares with Mahayana, the goal of attaining the enlightenment that leads to Buddhahood, but largely rejects devotional rituals and outward show. Instead, a Zen Buddhist believes that insight into 'Buddha nature' can be achieved by living rigorously according to the principles of Buddhism, and especially through meditation under the guidance of a Zen teacher. Central to this discipline is *zazen*, regular quiet meditation. Rather than seeking knowledge from texts or reaching a meditative state through ritual, Zen takes a more intellectual approach, encouraging practitioners to reach a true understanding through focused concentration.

Japanese Zen gardens arrange rocks, gravel and other natural elements in ways that serve as an aid to meditation.

Religion in ancient China

By the sixth century BCE, a sophisticated civil society had become established in the Chinese Empire. Until then, there had been a number of traditional 'folk religions' across China, with some shared beliefs and mythology, but as the country became a more unified civilization new religious ideas evolved. Influenced by the very structured nature of Chinese society under successive dynasties, these new belief systems shifted the emphasis from mythology and the worship of gods to questions of morality and what constitutes a 'good life'.

Learning and wisdom were valued highly, and respected scholars of history and philosophy such as Laozi and Confucius presented new ways of interpreting the world and our place in it. At much the same time, Buddha's teachings in India moved the emphasis from worship to lifestyle and morality, and these too soon spread into China. The old religions did not disappear, but continued alongside the newer, more philosophical belief systems of Daoism, Confucianism and, later, Buddhism.

#-0-1-2-3-4-5-6-7-8-9

0-
1-
2-
3-
4-
5-
6-

Dating from around 1000 BCE, the oracular *I Ching*, or *Book of Changes*, was a foundational text in both Daoism and Confucianism.

Laozi

China, under the emperors of the Zhou Dynasty, was a highly literate society and scholars were given important roles as librarians and archivists in the imperial courts. One who was particularly revered was known as Laozi, the 'Old Master', whose thoughts and teachings were recorded in a book titled *Dao De Jing*, 'The Way of Life'. This anthology of the scholar's sayings laid out a comprehensive religious philosophy, Daoism, based on following an eternal and unchanging way of life.

Little is known of Laozi's life, or even whether he actually existed. According to tradition, however, he became disappointed with the moral decline of the Zhou court in Chengzhou, and left on a water buffalo to travel around China living a simple life of solitude. At the gate to the city, so the story goes, a guard named Yinxi would not permit him to go without leaving behind some of his wisdom. Laozi obliged by writing the *Dao Do Jing* there and then, after which, he left, never to be seen again.

老子

Daoism

Laozi arrived at his philosophy of Daoism (sometimes 'Taoism') after long contemplation of the forces of nature and how they balance one another harmoniously. He was immersed in the traditional Chinese belief in a duality of yin and yang elements: feminine and masculine, dark and light, cold and warm.

He came to realize that there is an underlying principle to everything in the Universe, which he called *dao* (the way). *Dao* is eternal and unchanging, but we humans have tried with our material lifestyles and selfish ambitions to overcome it. Instead, we should endeavour to understand it and live according to the natural way of the Universe. Laozi advocated living a simple, contemplative life in accord with nature, renouncing the material world and emotional attachments. The idea was simple, but revolutionary in having no reference to deities. Daoism was at first considered a philosophical idea, but with its meditative practices soon gained a religious following, and was officially recognized as a religion during the Han Dynasty (206–220 CE).

Daoist temple on
Dragon Head Mountain
in China's Jilin province

Confucianism

L ike Laozi (see page 172), Confucius was employed as a scholar in the imperial courts of China, and was similarly dismayed by the descent into territorial rivalry under the Zhou Dynasty. But instead of turning his back on Chinese society as Laozi had done, he proposed a philosophy that he hoped could transform it.

Confucius set out a framework for society that would allow people to live in virtue and peace, and in harmony with one another rather than with nature. He became known as Kong Fuzi ('Master Kong', which became Westernized as Confucius) in deference to his wisdom, and in particular for his suggestion of returning to the old values of respect and loyalty under a benevolent leader, which he thought of as the 'way of heaven'.

Confucius also believed in scrupulously observing social niceties and following the rules of etiquette. It was this ritual aspect of his philosophy that led to Confucianism later being regarded as a religion.

The Mandate of Heaven

In Confucius's time, it was generally accepted that the ruling class, and the emperors in particular, governed by divine right and were morally superior to the masses. Confucius was a mere civil servant from a humble family, and when he looked at the state of Chinese society, he questioned that assumption.

He did not dismiss the notion of gods, nor the idea that morality and order have supernatural, heavenly origins. It was taken for granted that that was the case, but this was in a way irrelevant to Confucius's thinking. While he accepted that morality – that which is good and bad – is decided by heaven, he rejected the idea that the 'Mandate of Heaven' was only conferred on selected dynastic families, and the quality of virtue restricted to the aristocracy. Everyone, he argued, can learn the principles of goodness, and by practising them lead a virtuous life. In turn, this would be to the benefit of the whole of society. Rather than receiving virtue as a gift from heaven, Confucius argued, their virtuous behaviour would earn them the blessing of heaven.

Chinese emperors such as Fu Hsu took their authority from the gods — a claim that Confucius questioned.

Confucian ritual

As a servant of the imperial court, Confucius was anxious to show how his ideas could be put into practice for the good of the community. He suggested that the traditional virtues of loyalty and respect, if universally observed, would lead to greater social cohesion, as well as more morally correct behaviour. He also felt that these are best taught by example.

Society, Confucius argued, consists of various two-way relationships, such as between ruler and subject, father and son, husband and wife, elder and younger brothers, or older and younger friends. Confucius argued that the parties in these relationships can show loyalty to one another – the subject by showing respect to the ruler, and the ruler by his benevolence to his subject – according to a 'Golden Rule' of reciprocity: 'Do not do to others that which you would not like them to do to you'. To reinforce these mutually respectful relationships, Confucius placed great importance on a culture of strict etiquette and formalized rituals and ceremonies.

Elaborate traditional rituals at a Confucian temple in South Korea

Shinto

The indigenous religion of the Japanese people, Shinto, has evolved from the many different ancient folk religions of the islands of Japan. Some time in the eighth century, these diverse religions started to become unified under the name Shinto. They adopted similar rituals and ceremonies, and a standard dress code and style of shrine, while maintaining a variety of beliefs.

Shinto is, in essence, a form of animism, a belief that animals, plants and even inanimate objects possess a spirit, known as a *kami*. Shrines built to house these *kami* are also places of worship – generally, a formalized ritual practice in which offerings are made to the spirits. Today, while only a small percentage of people belong to organized Shinto sects, the majority of the Japanese population still adheres to traditional Shinto beliefs, and the distinctive Shinto shrine with its *torii* gateway remains as much a part of the Japanese landscape as the church is in Europe.

Traditional *torii* gate at the Shinto shrine on the island of Itsukushima.

Way of the Gods

As the various indigenous folk religions of Japan became unified in a single religious tradition, the word Shinto (Way of the Gods) was adopted. These 'gods' are personifications of natural phenomena – such as Amaterasu, the Sun goddess, and Fujin, the god of the wind – and are recognized as creators of the world.

The main focus of Shinto, however, is not on the creator gods, but on the *kami* (see page 182), more accurately described as spirits. They represent the spiritual essence or energy that is possessed by each living thing and some inanimate objects and places. The souls of the dead are also believed to live on as *kami*. The *kami* is the natural force inherent in something, rather than a supernatural being distinct from it. It inhabits this world rather than a separate realm, allowing an interaction between humans and the spirits. In this way followers of Shinto believe they can retain the connection with their ancestral past, and become conscious of humans' place as a part of an interconnected natural Universe.

Amaterasu emerges
from a tree.

Shinto rituals

The Shinto shrine, housing one or more particular *kami*, is the primary focus of acts of worship. The shrine itself may be within a temple building – typically, with a *torii* gateway symbolizing the threshold between the profane and the sacred – or even a complex of buildings. Many Shinto homes have miniature shrines, too, which are used for domestic worship.

Regardless as to whether the ceremony is conducted at home or in the worship hall of a temple, it normally follows a standard sequence of rites. The first is an act of ritual purification, which can range from simple washing of the hands or rinsing of the mouth to a cleansing of the whole body. The worshipper will then make an offering to the *kami* – typically of food such as fruit, vegetables or rice – to maintain harmony between humans and the *kami*, and to ensure the goodwill of the gods. This is followed by bowing twice in front of the shrine to honour the *kami*, and clapping hands twice before starting a period of prayer. The ceremony concludes with a final bow to the shrine.

A Shinto priest brandishes a harai-gushi purification wand.

Amulets and talismans

The offerings made during Shinto worship are not made simply to honour or propitiate the spirits and gods, but are also often associated with prayers asking for their favour.

The *kami* and human affairs are believed to be interrelated, and followers of Shinto use different talismans when making requests for spirit intervention. In many Shinto temples, for example, there is a wall reserved for displaying *ema*, small flat wooden tokens bearing a picture or symbol. A person can write a message to an appropriate *kami* on one of these, expressing a wish, and asking for help in almost any aspect of their life. Today, many of these *ema* are commercially produced, and designed for specific requests, such as success in an exam, promotion at work or even finding a romantic partner. At many shrines, worshippers can also buy talismans called *ofuda*, bearing the name of a *kami* that is believed to protect the home of the bearer, or *omamori*, personal amulets that bring good fortune and health.

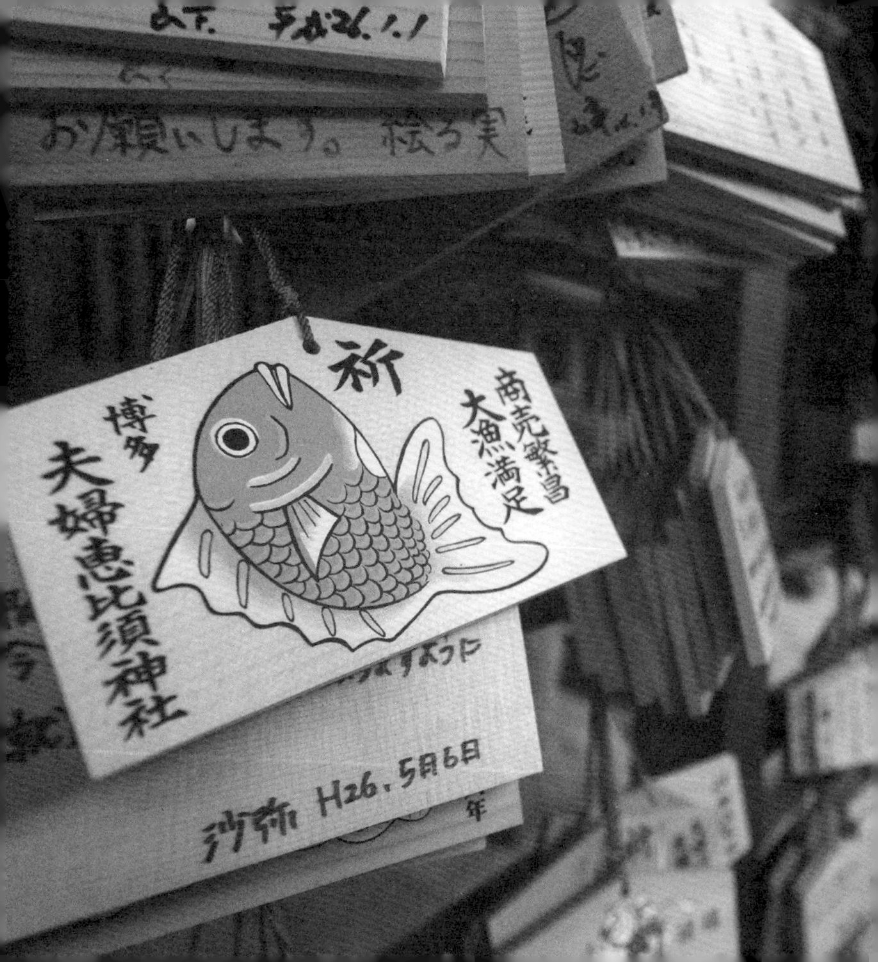
お願いします。
祈
博多
夫婦恵比須神社
商売繁昌
大漁満足
H26. 5月6日

Judaism

One of the oldest monotheistic religions, Judaism has its roots in the religion of the Semitic people of the southern Levant more than 3,000 years ago. This area, known as Canaan, became the home of the descendants of Abraham, the Children of Israel, who believed they had been given the land in a covenant granted by God. Judaism is therefore closely linked to the history of the Jewish people, and the core belief in a special relationship between them and God.

The story is related in the Hebrew Bible (see page 206). Throughout history, however, the Jewish people have been driven out of their Promised Land, and forced into exile where they have often faced persecution. The connection with the land of Israel is strong, however. In modern times, the political Zionist movement led to the eventual establishment of a Jewish homeland in Israel, but only after the extermination of millions by the Nazis. Today there are 14 million Jewish people across the globe, although not all are practising religious Jews.

The Patriarchs

According to the Hebrew Bible, the ancestry of the Jewish people can be traced back to a single family line, known as the Patriarchs. In a broad sense, these are the direct descendants of Adam, the first man. More specifically in Judaism, however, the term 'Patriarch' usually refers to Abraham, his son Isaac and grandson Jacob, who are believed to have lived from about 2000 BCE.

Abraham was called upon by God to leave his family and settle in Canaan, where he was prophesied to be the father of a great people. But his wife Sarah was unable to conceive, and Abraham fathered a son Ishmael with her Egyptian maid Hagar. Abraham despaired of having a legitimate heir, so God interceded and Sarah became pregnant. Their son Isaac inherited Abraham's claim to the land, which in turn passed to his son Jacob. With his wives Rachel and Leah, and their handmaidens Bilhah and Zilpah, Jacob fathered twelve sons, the progenitors of the Tribes of Israel and ancestors of the Jewish people.

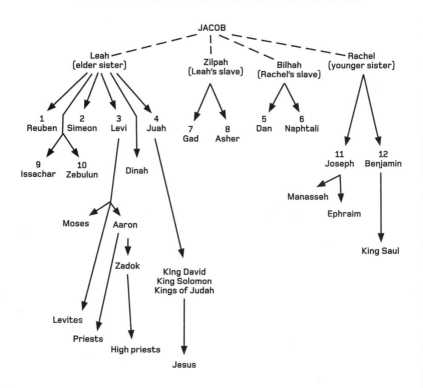

The twelve sons of Jacob and the tribes of Israel

God's covenant and the Promised Land

A central belief of Judaism is that there is only one God, the creator of the world and the people in it, who keeps a watchful eye on His creation. At one stage, God was so enraged by the behaviour of the people that He decided to destroy them all with a worldwide flood. But He then relented, making an agreement or covenant with Noah that allowed him to save his own family and pairs of all creatures to repopulate the world after it had been cleansed by the flood (opposite).

While the covenant with Noah was made to save all humankind, later agreements were specifically between God and the Children of Israel, whom God regarded as His chosen people. The first, and most important, was with the Patriarch Abraham. God promised Abraham that in return for their obedience to His laws, his descendants would become a great nation occupying the land of Canaan. God's covenant with Abraham is the foundation of both the Jewish people and the religion of Judaism, and the origin of their claim to the 'Promised Land'.

Moses and the Ten Commandments

Although Canaan had been promised to Abraham and his heirs, a severe drought forced Jacob and his family to move to Egypt. Offering refuge at first, the pharaohs later enslaved the Israelites for fear of an uprising. Moses, a survivor of an Egyptian purge of newborn Israelites, was called upon by God to lead his people back to Canaan.

Negotiations with the pharaoh for their release came to nothing. In his anger, God caused a series of plagues in Egypt, and the pharaoh relented. With God's help, Moses parted the Red Sea to allow the Israelites to cross, pursued by the pharaoh's army, who were drowned when the waters flowed back. The Israelites were now on their way to Canaan. Moses climbed Mount Sinai where he spent 40 days and 40 nights. During this time, God gave him the laws for the Jewish people, the Ten Commandments, and the foundations of the Torah, the first part of the Hebrew Bible. These laws are the terms of the covenant between God and Moses, in return for his delivering the Israelites from Egypt.

לא תרצח :   אנכי " אלהיך
No mates   Yo. A. tu dios que-

לא תנאף :   לא יהיה לך
No forniques   No sea a ti dioses-

לא תגנב :   לא תשא את
No hurtes   No jures a nombre-

לא תענה   זכור את יום
No atestigues   Miembra a dia del-

לא תחמד   כבר את אביך
No codicies   Honra a tu padre-

Moses and his brother Aaron with the
tablets of the Ten Commandments

The Messiah

Once Moses had led the Israelites out of enslavement in Egypt (see page 196), they settled in Canaan once more. Several generations later, however, the neighbouring Philistines had repeatedly attacked and taken their territory, and morale was at a low ebb. To restore order, the Israelites appointed Saul as their king, but put pressure on him to disobey God's rule.

God commanded Saul to abdicate in favour of David, who was to be anointed with holy oil as a sign of his spiritual, as well as political, leadership. Because of this, David became known as Messiah (the anointed one), the prophesied priest and king who would be saviour of the Jewish people. Just as David had been sent by God to rescue and rule the Israelites when they lost faith and were under attack, it is believed in Judaism that another Messiah will come to the aid of the Jews. It is prophesied that this future Messiah, a descendant of David, will unite the Tribes of Israel and bring the Jewish people together in the land of Eretz Israel.

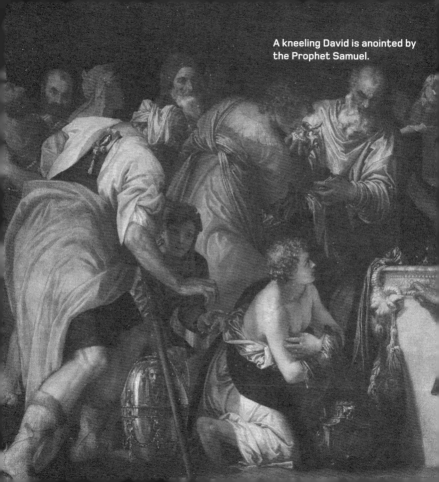

A kneeling David is anointed by the Prophet Samuel.

Jerusalem and the temple

In their forty-year exodus from Egypt, the Israelites became nomads. They had no permanent dwellings or place of worship. They constructed a portable temple, the Tabernacle, from boards and cloths decorated with gold, jewels and other valuables that they had taken with them from Egypt. The Tabernacle became an important symbol of their faith and remained in use after their arrival in Canaan.

When David was anointed king, he decreed that his son Solomon would build a temple in Jerusalem, a centre for the Jewish people and their religion. The First Temple, therefore, had considerable significance, and its destruction by Babylonian invaders in the sixth century BCE was a severe blow. A Second Temple was built after the fall of the Babylonians, but once again invasion – this time by the Romans – saw its destruction in 70 CE. Following the Islamic conquest of Jerusalem in the seventh century, the Dome of the Rock and al-Aqsa Mosque were built on the site of the original temple, the Temple Mount.

The diaspora

Following failed revolts against Roman occupation in 70 CE and again in 135 CE, the Jewish people were driven out of the land then known as Judea (once Moses's promised land of Canaan). This marked the beginning of a long exile for all Jewish people. Without their homeland, they became a diaspora, which over time became scattered across the Middle East, North Africa and Europe.

A minority of Jews remained in the former Roman province of Palestine and countries that were later to become Islamic, but many headed north in medieval times to France and Germany, or to central and Eastern Europe. The Ashkenazim, as they became known, were treated with suspicion by many of their host countries, and did not integrate easily. Many settled in often isolated communities, where they developed a distinctive culture and interpretation of Judaism, as well as their own language, Yiddish. A somewhat smaller number of Jews, the Sephardim, settled in Spain and Portugal, but were forced either to flee to North Africa or convert to Christianity after Spanish Catholics regained southern Spain from the Muslims.

Routes of the
Jewish diaspora
from the first to
sixteenth centuries

ENGLAND

RUSSIA

POLAND

GERMANIC
LANDS

FRANCE

SPAIN

GREECE

BYZANTIUM

PORTUGAL

TUNISIA

JUDEA

EGYPT

——— Migrations

- - - - - - - Expulsions

The Torah

As part of his covenant with Moses (see page 196), God gave him the Ten Commandments on tablets of stone, with instructions that these be kept in a specially made container, the Ark of the Covenant. The Israelites carried the Ark with them for the remainder of their journey to Canaan, giving it pride of place in the Tabernacle wherever they camped.

God is also believed to have revealed the texts of the Torah – the first part of the Jewish holy scriptures – to Moses on Mount Sinai, or later in the Tabernacle. The Torah, meaning 'instruction' or 'guidance' in Hebrew, is considered to be the word of God. As well as expanding on the commandments at the heart of the covenant, the Torah tells the story of the Creation and events leading up to the foundation of the Jewish people. There are five parts to the Torah – Genesis, Exodus, Leviticus, Numbers and Deuteronomy, known in Hebrew as Bereishit, Shemot, Vayikra, Bemidbar and Devarim – sometimes referred to by the Greek word Pentateuch (the five scrolls).

The Hebrew Bible

The Torah (see page 204) forms the first part of the Tanakh, the Hebrew Bible. In addition to the five books of the Torah, there are two further parts, the Nevi'im and the Ketuvim.

The Nevi'im comprises the books of the prophets (the Former Prophets Joshua, Judges, Samuel and Kings; the Latter Prophets Isaiah, Jeremiah and Ezekiel; and the 12 minor prophets), continuing the narrative of God's relationship with the Jewish people begun in the Torah. The Ketuvim (Writings) is a collection of miscellaneous divinely inspired texts, by various authors who do not have the same authority as the prophets. The Tanakh is also supplemented by commentaries on and interpretations of the holy texts, which are derived from the Oral Torah, a body of knowledge passed down for centuries and collected as the Talmud and the Midrash. The Talmud has a particular authority in Judaism, as it is the result of the cumulative wisdom of generations of Jewish scholars – the rabbis – concerning the laws, customs and history of Judaism.

אנכי ה״
לא יהיה לך
לא תשא
זכור את
כבד את
לא תרצח
לא תנאף
לא תגנב
לא תענה
לא תחמד

The Kabbalah

For some Jews the traditional interpretations of the Torah provided an intellectual framework for their beliefs, but lacked any mysticism. To supplement these rather prosaic commentaries, a number of scholars sought a more mystical approach, which offered an esoteric cosmology – the Kabbalah.

The first written exposition of these ideas was the Zohar (Divine Splendour), compiled in Spain in the 13th century and popularized by Rabbi Isaac Luria some 300 years later. Dealing with such philosophical questions as the nature of the Universe and the meaning of human existence, the Kabbalah provided a new spiritual dimension to Judaism. In particular, it explained the relationship between the eternal infinity, Ein Sof, with the finite Universe and the mortal beings within it. The nature of the divine is described by means of ten Sephirot (attributes) and likened to a single light in ten separate vessels. The idea of reuniting these ten 'divine sparks' to repair the damage in the world particularly appealed to the Jewish people scattered in exile.

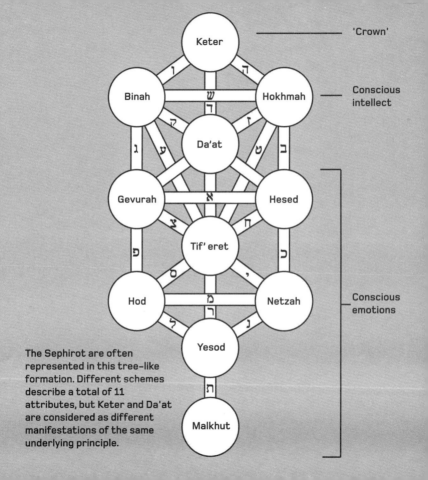

The Sephirot are often represented in this tree-like formation. Different schemes describe a total of 11 attributes, but Keter and Da'at are considered as different manifestations of the same underlying principle.

Rabbis

Until the destruction of the Second Temple of Jerusalem (see page 200), a hereditary class of priests played an important role in the practice of Judaism. But with the removal of their central focus, the position became largely honorary, and the role of the priest as a leader of worship virtually disappeared.

Ceremonies could be performed without the need for professional clergy, and the traditional authority they held passed to rabbis – the scholars and teachers responsible for interpretating Jewish law. In time, the rabbis acquired a more pastoral role, especially in the isolated communities of the diaspora, and participated in services by giving sermons and, in some cases, leading the prayers. It is still not the rabbi's duty to conduct religious ceremonies though, and this can be done by any adult man or (in some denominations) woman from the congregation. He or she can be nominated as the *shatz* (prayer leader) or the *baal kriyah* (reader of a passage from the Torah).

Service of the heart

The Talmud, the rabbinical interpretation of the instructions of the Torah, stresses the importance of prayer in Jewish worship, describing it as the 'service of the heart'. It is the central element of the Jewish liturgy, along with readings from the Torah.

The *siddur*, the Jewish prayer book, contains prayers for various occasions and the most important of these is the Amidah (standing prayer), which is the focus of the service of worship. Also known as the Shemoneh Esrei (18 blessings), the Amidah actually has 19 verses, but can be modified to suit various occasions. The Shema Yisrael, a verse from the Torah, is also normally recited as a declaration of faith: 'Hear, O Israel! The Lord is our God! The Lord is One!' Devout Jews will pray three times a day, or more on the Shabbat (day of rest) and festivals, but it is not compulsory to attend a synagogue for communal worship. Only certain activities, such as reading from the Torah, reciting the Birkat Hamazon (grace after meals), or weddings and funerals require a *minyan* – a quorum of ten adult Jews.

The synagogue

Although not necessary for worship, the synagogue plays a role in many Jewish communities. Loosely modelled on the Tabernacle and temples of antiquity, synagogues vary in architectural style and go by various names. In Israel, the synagogue is known as Beit Knesset (house of assembly); to Ashkenazim, it is referred to as the *shul*; and in many progressive denominations it is simply the temple.

A typical synagogue may consist of a main sanctuary for prayer and additional rooms for study and community uses. In most, there is an ark containing the scrolls of the Torah, often housed behind a decorative curtain. Facing this – and also facing the direction of Jerusalem – is the *amud*, the pulpit for the prayer leader, and a *bimah*, a table from which the Torah is read. There is generally a lantern that is kept continually lit, symbolizing the perpetual light of the menorah in the temple of Jerusalem (see page 224). There may also be a *mikveh* attached to the synagogue – a bath for ritual cleansing.

Jewish festivals

Observance of Shabbat, from sunset on Friday to sunset on Saturday, is required by Jewish law as one of the Ten Commandments. During this weekly remembrance of God's day of rest and the Exodus of the Hebrews from Egypt, work (in its broadest sense) is forbidden, and Jews celebrate with prayers, lighting of candles and three special festive meals.

The Jewish calendar contains several festivals commemorating events in its religious history. Pesach (Passover) is a week-long festival celebrating the Exodus, and in particular the 'passing over' of Jewish children when God's tenth plague inflicted death to the first-born children in Egypt. Shavuot (Festival of Weeks) remembers God's gift of the Commandments to Moses. Sukkot (Festival of Tabernacles) gives thanks for God's protection of the Israelites during their flight from Egypt. The Jewish New Year is celebrated as Rosh Hashanah, a ten-day period of remembrance and repentance leading up to Yom Kippur, the Day of Atonement.

A man blows the ceremonial *shofar* ram's horn during Rosh Hashanah

Rites of passage

Like many religions, Judaism marks the important stages of a person's life with ceremonies and rituals that strengthen his or her ties with the community.

The first of these for male Jews is *brit milah*, on the eighth day after birth, in which the child is named and circumcized. This is a symbol of God's covenant with Abraham. There is a less common name-giving ceremony, *brit bat*, for girls. At the age of 12 or 13, Jewish boys celebrate their coming of age in their *bar mitzvah* (12-year-old girls may have a similar ceremony), when they are welcomed into the congregation. Jewish weddings are imbued with religious significance; following a ceremony beneath a decorated canopy, the groom stamps on a glass in remembrance of the destruction of the temple and the dispersing of the Jewish people. Funerals, held as soon as possible after death, are invariably burials and not cremations. There are strict rules concerning the preparation of the body, the prayers offered and even the three stages of mourning.

A Jewish boy holds the Torah scrolls during his *bar mitzvah* celebrations.

Women and Judaism

Until comparatively recently, there has been a division in the roles of the sexes in Judaism. Women have an unusual status, as the rabbinical ruling is that a person who is the child of a Jewish mother, not father, inherits the identity of being a Jew.

In other ways, however, women have not traditionally been accorded the same rights as men, and remain excluded from certain privileges in some orthodox denominations. For example, while not excluded from religious services, women were traditionally partitioned into separate areas of the synagogue, usually at the back, and not permitted to participate by reading from the Torah or leading prayers. Similarly, the *minyan* (see page 212) was exclusively ten males. However, since the advent of progressive movements in Judaism during the 19th century, women have won a considerable degree of equality, especially in the Reform and Conservative branches of the religion (see page 232). Today, they can be active members of their congregations, and even ordained as rabbis.

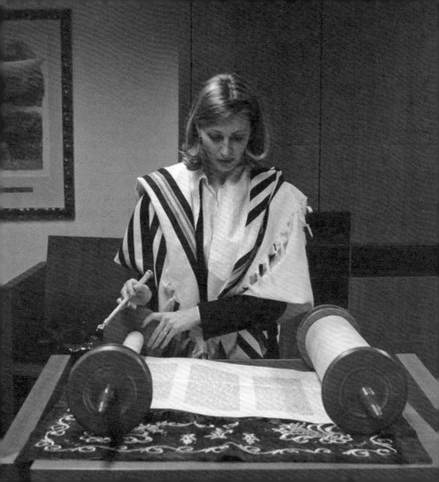

Kosher food

The Torah contains a multitude of laws that observant Jews accept without question as the terms of God's covenant with them. Among them are the *kashrut* – the dietary rules laid out mainly in the books of Leviticus and Deuteronomy that determine what is kosher or acceptable in Jewish law.

These specify the animals that are considered unclean, and therefore forbidden, such as insects other than some locusts, shellfish, reptiles, amphibians and pigs (which, although having cloven hooves, are not ruminants). There are also strict instructions on the method of slaughter, *shechita*, which has to be carried out by a trained professional by completely cutting the throat of the animal in one swift movement using a sharp blade. The body then has to be completely drained and cleaned of any trace of blood. It is forbidden to mix meat and dairy products or to serve them together in the same meal. Many Jewish households have different storage areas for meat and milk products, and even separate cooking utensils and dishes.

A traditional kosher Passover meal, including stuffed *gefilte* fish, *tsimmes* stew, red wine and *matzah* flatbreads

Signs and symbols

The menorah, the seven-branched candlestick, has been used as a symbol of Judaism since the time of the Exodus. It is said that God instructed Moses to make a menorah to give light in the Tabernacle, and to represent the faith of the Jewish people. The menorah subsequently became a focal point of ceremonies in the Temple in Jerusalem.

Another widespread symbol is the six-pointed Star of David. Originating as a Kabbalistic symbol of protection, it has become associated in particular with the Zionist movement and the nation of Israel. Several items of clothing have symbolic significance. These include the *kippah* (known by Ashkenazim as a *yarmulke*), the skull cap that men wear, especially when praying, studying the Torah or eating, and the *tallit*, the prayer shawl with its distinctive tassels. Some orthodox branches of Judaism, such as Hasidism (see page 228), have a stricter dress code for headgear and coats, and the wearing of *payot* – curled ringlets of hair at the temples.

Depiction of the menorah on the Arch of Titus in Rome

Orthodox Judaism

Over the centuries, several movements have evolved from the rabbinic Judaism that gave the authoritative commentaries and interpretations of the Torah. In modern times, challenges from progressive movements such as Reform and Conservative Judaism have led to a broader spectrum of Jewish beliefs (see page 232). However, the central denomination, known as Orthodox Judaism, continues to accept the rabbis' assertion that God revealed both the written and oral Torah to Moses and that, as the word of God, the laws in them are unchangeable and must be strictly followed.

The strictest Orthodox denominations, sometimes pejoratively known as 'ultra orthodox', include Haredi Judaism and Hasidism, but there is also a more liberal movement known as Modern Orthodox Judaism. Today, Orthodox Judaism is considered to be a traditionalist movement within the Jewish faith, and has its largest following in Israel, while in North America only about 10 per cent of Jews identify themselves as Orthodox.

Hasidism

Among the Jews of the diaspora, the Ashkenazim in northern and central Europe settled in rural villages they called *shtetls*, with tight-knit social structures. Their shared Jewish faith was an important part of these communities, but there was a feeling that the formulaic prayers and readings of traditional Judaism did not provide the inspiration they needed.

A movement known as Hasidism evolved, offering more inclusive participation in worship, including singing and dancing and a generally more ecstatic experience. The rabbi, traditionally a scholarly figure, took on a different role and was seen as a father-figure to the community, actively involved with village life, as well as an inspirational spiritual leader. The celebratory aspects of Hasidism proved popular, and from its beginnings in 18th-century Ukraine it spread across much of the Jewish world. Observant Hasidic men, often wearing long beards and side curls, are recognizable by their distinctive long coats and large hats harking back to their Eastern European origins.

Sephardic Judaism

Sephardic Jews developed their own distinctive form of Judaism. Under Moorish rule in southern Spain, they absorbed several aspects of Islamic culture. Their Judaism tended to be mystical, exploring ideas of the Kabbalah (see page 208), but also more philosophical, thanks to an atmosphere of studying classical texts fostered by Islamic scholars.

The Jewish thinker Moses Maimonides (1135–1204) was a product of this cross-fertilization of cultures, proposing the definitive 13 principles of Jewish faith that are still referenced today. When the Spanish conquered the Muslims and regained all of Spain, the Inquisition also wanted to remove the Jews. Many fled for North Africa, the Middle East and Europe. Unlike the Ashkenazim, who had developed their conservatively Orthodox Hasidic Judaism in isolated rural communities (see page 228), the Sephardic Jews were more liberal and more accustomed to urban life. They integrated more easily into the secular and especially commercial life of their host countries.

Modernizing Judaism

Life in Europe changed dramatically during the 18th century. Society became more prosperous with increased international trade and scientific discoveries, and the authority of monarchies and religious institutions was being challenged. But Jewish communities were conservative and reluctant to accept change.

The philosopher Moses Mendelssohn argued for a Haskalah (Jewish Enlightenment), and for Jews to assimilate themselves into modern society. This was the beginning of a progressive movement that, in the 19th century, generated a number of new denominations. Reform Judaism developed in Germany, rejecting the idea that Jewish laws are eternal and unchanging. It offered a more liberal form of religious service without segregation of the sexes, and proposed more liberal interpretations of the spirit of the laws. Generally, Orthodox Jews rejected the Reform movement, though some who had sympathy with the ideas, but felt they went too far, established a Conservative Judaism movement that is particularly widespread in North America.

Logo of the Union for Reform Judaism

Zionism

The Jews in Europe frequently suffered discrimination and persecution – a problem that was exacerbated by the reluctance of some to integrate into the culture of their adopted countries. By the 19th century, the situation had become identified as 'the Jewish question'. While many believed that assimilation was the answer to the problem, some realized that they faced anti-Semitism no matter how hard they tried.

In his book, *The Jewish State* (1896), Theodor Herzl argued that the answer was to establish a Jewish homeland. This, of course, had echoes of the historical return of the Jewish people to Israel, and the natural choice for this new nation was the 'Holy Land', then part of Palestine ruled by the Ottoman Empire. Hertzl's ideas soon caught on, prompting the establishment of Zionism, a political movement pressing for international agreement to the foundation of a Jewish nation. This was eventually achieved In the wake of the Nazi Holocaust, when the State of Israel was formally established in 1948.

The Jewish identity

Judaism, it is often asserted, is a religion, not a nationality, yet there is more to identifying oneself as a Jew than religion, or being a citizen of the State of Israel. Certainly, all followers of Judaism would consider themselves to be Jewish, but there are many Jews who do not identify with the Jewish faith.

The concept of 'Jewishness' is hotly debated: the traditional view is that Jews are an ethno-religious group, strictly speaking the descendants of the Patriarchs (see page 192) who share the beliefs of Judaism. But nonreligious Jews would argue that the defining characteristics are ethno-social, and that Jews have a common ancestry and culture, rather than religion. Because the Jewish people have spent so much of their history in exile, permanent immigrants in their adopted countries, they have developed a distinctive culture alongside their religion, with its own languages – Yiddish, for example – food, music and even comedy, giving them a complex identity with a unique status among the peoples of the world.

Persecution

Once driven out of Israel by the Romans, the Jewish people were scattered around the world. Because of their religion and, to some extent, appearance they were regarded as alien in many places, and were often unable to find permanent homes.

Like other migrant people, they were viewed with hostility, but perhaps more than any other group they suffered persecution for their ethnicity. Anti-Semitism, rife across Europe, meant that it was often impossible for Jews to integrate into society, and especially to find employment. Consequently, many became entrepreneurs, merchants, traders and moneylenders. Such activities fuelled further anti-Semitic feeling, which reached murderous proportions in the pogroms of Russia and Ukraine in the 19th century, and the genocidal extermination of millions of Jews by the Nazis in the 20th century. Even today, only 17 per cent of Jews live outside Israel or North America, and some far-right political groups in Europe and the US continue to hold openly anti-Semitic views.

Christianity

About one-third of the world's population – more than 2.3 billion people – consider themselves Christian, making Christianity by far the largest religion today. The religion evolved from a small Jewish sect in Roman-occupied Judea around 2,000 years ago, who believed that a man called Jesus was the Messiah prophesied in the Hebrew Bible (see page 206).

Jesus's life and teachings were recorded by his followers in the books now known collectively as the New Testament, and are the basis for the main beliefs and practices of Christianity. Central to these beliefs is that Jesus was not a prophet, but the God incarnate – both human and divine – who came to Earth, died and was resurrected. Another distinctive belief of Christianity is in the Trinity, that there is only one God, but He exists in three distinct forms: the Father, the Son and the Holy Spirit. Initially suppressed by the Romans, Christianity gained many converts and soon became the predominant religion of Europe. Today it is the major faith in most countries of Europe and the Americas.

The Chi-Rho monogram combining two Greek letters is one of the oldest Christian symbols.

A New Covenant

Jesus was born in Bethlehem, in what was then the Roman province of Judea, and his first followers were Jews. They regarded him as the fulfilment of a prophecy in the Tanakh that God would one day send a Messiah to save the world. His arrival was regarded not so much as a rejection of the old beliefs as a continuation of them.

The first Christians retained many beliefs and practices of Judaism, including the rituals of worship and priesthood. But what distinguished the Christians most radically from the original Jewish faith was their belief that Jesus was not merely a prophet – or even the Messiah – but God in human form. For his followers, his coming signalled a new covenant with God, which was enshrined in the teachings of Jesus. Just as God's covenant with the Jewish people was recorded in the Torah, the new covenant was written in the books of the New Testament, adding to, rather than replacing, the Hebrew Bible (known by Christians as the Old Testament).

The inscription 'Jesus of Nazareth, King of the Jews', fixed on the cross prior to Christ's Crucifixion.

The Virgin birth

It is a central belief of Christianity that Jesus is both the prophesied Messiah and God incarnate. He was born in the fourth century BCE, to a young Jewish couple, Joseph and Mary, who had travelled to Bethlehem to register for the Roman taxes.

Christians believe that Mary was a virgin, who had been told by the angel Gabriel that she would miraculously conceive a child whose father was God himself. This child, the Son of God, would be both truly God and truly man. Bethlehem was crowded with people registering for the census, and the only accommodation available for the heavily pregnant Mary was a stable, where the child was born and recognized by three 'wise men' as the Messiah.

As the Mother of God, Mary is considered a saint and has a very special status in many branches of Christianity. The Virgin Mary, or the Madonna, is especially venerated by Roman Catholics, who revere her above all other saints and address many of their prayers to her.

Jesus Christ

Despite the claim that Jesus was the Messiah, the heir to David's throne as King of the Jews, he was born to a humble family from Nazareth, and followed his father in becoming a carpenter. His coming had been foretold by John the Baptist, a wandering preacher who became a religious guide to Jesus, and who baptized him in the river Jordan.

The baptism was a turning point for Jesus. It confirmed his status as the Messiah and Son of God and marked the beginning of his ministry. Following a 40-day period of solitude in the desert, in which he resisted the temptations of the devil, he too became an itinerant preacher, gathering around him a group of close disciples. But his activities were seen as subversive by both the Roman authorities and the Jewish priesthood, and he was eventually arrested and sentenced to death by crucifixion. After a slow and painful death on the cross, Jesus miraculously came to life again, and spent 40 days among his followers before ascending into heaven.

The teachings of Jesus

The Jewish priests regarded Jesus as a heretical preacher leading a breakaway sect, yet his message was very similar to the teachings of Judaism: the love of God and of humanity.

He began his preaching in the area around the Sea of Galilee, where he slowly acquired a following, including the first disciples. His reputation as a preacher was firmly established when he addressed a crowd from a hill near Galilee, in what came to be known as the Sermon on the Mount. Illustrating his message with parables, conducting healing sessions and performing miracles such as walking on water, Jesus became famous as he travelled across Judea. On arrival in Jerusalem, he was greeted by huge crowds, but chose to ride into the city on a humble donkey. Here he clashed with the Jewish priests, exposing their hypocrisy by driving moneylenders out of the temple and challenging their authority. After only a short period of preaching, he had become a threat to the priests and an annoyance to the Roman rulers of Judea.

Ruins of the synagogue at Capernaum, one of the sites where Jesus preached.

Jesus's disciples

In the short period he spent as an itinerant preacher, Jesus amassed a considerable following, including a loyal band of disciples, who travelled with him, helping to spread the word of his ministry. Even from the beginning of his preaching, Jesus made close friendships with a number of these disciples, some of whom had been followers of John the Baptist.

In all, Jesus recruited 12 of these trusted friends, also known as the Apostles, to accompany him. The first were two fishermen from Galilee: Simon, whom he called Peter, his rock (from the Greek *petros*, meaning 'rock'), and his brother Andrew. They were joined by two other fishermen, James and John, also brothers. Philip, Bartholomew, Thomas, Matthew, James, Thaddeus (also known as Jude), Simon and Judas Iscariot joined later. After Jesus's death, the disciples, along with Paul, a thirteenth disciple called by Jesus after his resurrection, continued to promote his teachings, and laid the foundations of the Christian Church.

The New Testament

As an Abrahamic religion with its roots in Judaism, Christianity accepts the authority of the Jewish Bible, which is known by Christians as the Old Testament. Added to it, however, are the specifically Christian scriptures that describe the life and teachings of Jesus – The New Testament.

The first four books of the New Testament, the Gospels, are biographical accounts of Jesus's life, believed to be records of the first-hand recollections of his Apostles. The four Gospels are traditionally ascribed to Matthew, Mark, Luke and John, although their authorship is a matter of scholarly debate. As well as telling the story of Jesus's life, with particular reference to his birth and death, the Gospels all give detailed accounts of his preaching, and transcriptions of his sermons and parables. The Gospels are followed by a description of the founding of the Christian Church after Jesus's resurrection, the Acts of the Apostles, and the Book of Revelation, a description of the Day of Judgement at the end of time.

The Last Supper

Following his clashes with the priests in the temple in Jerusalem, Jesus knew he would soon face punishment and even death. He gathered his 12 Apostles for one last meal together, in order to prepare them for their mission once he was gone. The events surrounding this Last Supper are described in great detail in all the Gospels, and have become central to the beliefs and practices of Christianity.

At the meal, Jesus offers his disciples bread, telling them that this is his body and that he will give it in sacrifice for the good of humanity. Afterwards, he washes their feet, saying that they are his friends, not his servants, and that they should love one another as he has loved them. Having explained to them the message he wants them to give to the world, he predicts that one of them will betray him (Judas Iscariot had in fact already secretly agreed to identify Jesus to the authorities), and that his most trusted friend Peter would deny all knowledge of Jesus three times before the cock crows next morning.

Jesus's crucifixion

After the Last Supper, Jesus was confronted by an angry crowd led by Judas who, with a kiss, identified him to the authorities. While Jesus was arrested and taken to face the Jewish court, his Apostles went into hiding. When questioned, Peter repeatedly denied any association with Jesus.

Exasperated by Jesus's calm defence of his claim to be the Messiah, the Jewish court sent him to the Roman governor Pontius Pilate and Herod Antipas, ruler of Galilee, charged with claiming to be the King of the Jews. Unable to make a decision, Pilate followed a Jewish custom, offering the people a choice of sparing either Jesus or a murderer called Barabbas. The crowd opted to free Barabbas, and Jesus was sentenced to death by crucifixion. He was taken to Golgotha where he was nailed to a cross and left to die. His body was taken down and sealed in a tomb, but three days later this was found empty. Resurrected from the dead, Jesus rejoined his Apostles for 40 days before ascending into heaven to sit at the right hand of God the Father.

The Holy Trinity

A distinguishing feature of Christianity is the acceptance of Jesus as God incarnate, the Son of God. However, this is only one aspect of a belief central to most mainstream Christian faiths – that one God exists in three distinct forms.

This would appear to contradict the idea inherited from Judaism that there is only one God, but the Christian doctrine of the Holy Trinity explains that the three persons referred to as God in the Bible are one and the same substance, simply manifested in different forms. From the perspective of monotheism, it is easy to understand God the Father as the almighty, the creator; God the Son, Jesus, is a more subtle concept and involves an embodiment of God that exists both before and after his incarnation. Similarly, the Holy Spirit is an aspect of God with its own distinct form, symbolically showing itself, for example, as a dove descending at Jesus's baptism, and as tongues of fire when Jesus's followers celebrated Pentecost 50 days after his resurrection.

The Last Judgement

In the Old Testament, there are references to the coming Messiah, a saviour of the Jewish people and all humankind, who will usher in an age of justice and peace. Christians believe that Jesus is the Messiah that was prophesied, and that he lived as a man and died on the cross for our salvation. They also believe that the Son of God will return to decide who shall be given eternal life or eternal punishment.

This Second Coming, graphically described in the Book of Revelation, will be announced by a trumpet call from the angels, which heralds the end of time. Then, all who have lived will be called to account: the dead will be raised from the Earth to join the living for the Last Judgement. Those who have accepted Jesus as the Son of God, and have demonstrated their goodness by their treatment of others, will be saved to live eternally in Heaven with God; those who have failed to love God, and to love their fellow humans, will be taken to an eternity of suffering in Hell.

Heaven and Hell

For Christians, the concept of the afterlife is closely linked to the apocalyptic vision of the Second Coming of the Son of God (see page 260). What happens to us following death is simply an intermediate stage, until we are resurrected and sent to our final destination.

The Christian Heaven is not explicitly described in the Bible, but is said to be where the souls of people who accept Christ and his teachings reside with God until the Last Judgement. God will then create a new Kingdom of Heaven on Earth where the saved will live eternally. Hell is the realm of Lucifer, the fallen angel. It is a place of punishment and suffering for souls separated from God. After resurrection, some people may be forgiven their sins if they have faith in Jesus's self-sacrifice for their salvation. Otherwise, they are condemned to eternal separation from the goodness of God. Various Christian denominations have different interpretations of the criteria for the final judgement, and the nature of the eternal afterlife.

The Last Judgement, by Hieronymus Bosch

The Eucharist

A central part of Christian worship is the rite of eating bread and drinking wine as the Apostles did at the Last Supper. Known as the Eucharist (from the Greek meaning 'thanksgiving'), the ritual's significance is derived from the description of Jesus breaking bread and giving it to his disciples with the words, 'This is my body, which is given for you' and giving them wine saying, 'This cup . . . is the new covenant in my blood'.

The Eucharist is the focal point of the Roman Catholic Mass, the Orthodox Divine Liturgy and many versions of the Protestant service of Holy Communion. Different branches of Christianity are divided over the question of transubstantiation – that is, whether the bread and wine literally become the body and blood of Jesus. Roman Catholics and most Eastern Orthodox Christians believe that there is a substantial change, and those taking communion actually receive Christ; most Protestant denominations regard the consuming of a wafer and wine merely as the symbolic observance of Jesus's covenant.

Baptism

Of the Christian rites of passage marking the key stages of a follower's life, the most important is baptism – a ritual cleansing by immersion in, or sprinkling with, water as a sign that the person is accepted as a follower of Jesus. The ceremony mimics Jesus's own baptism by John the Baptist, at which the Holy Spirit descended in the form of a dove, marking the beginning of his ministry (see page 246).

Also known as christening, especially when performed as part of a child's name-giving ceremony, baptism symbolically washes away the 'original sin' of Adam and Eve's disobedience, which is forgiven as part of Jesus's covenant with his followers. In some branches of Christianity, such as Roman Catholicism and Anglicanism, children are baptized as infants. They later go through a ceremony of confirmation, when they become full adult members of the Church. Other denominations believe that baptism should be preformed when a person is old enough to make the decision to become a member of the Church.

Christian festivals

The Christian calendar includes numerous festivals, most of which commemorate significant events in Jesus's life. On 25 December, Christmas celebrates the birth of Jesus in most branches of Christianity. In the Orthodox traditions, the event is not considered as important as Epiphany. Coming 12 days after Christmas, on 6 January, Epiphany celebrates the arrival of the wise men, and their declaration that Jesus was indeed the prophesied Messiah.

The events surrounding Christ's death and resurrection are also marked by festivals. Maundy Thursday commemorates the day of the Last Supper and is followed by Good Friday, the day of the crucifixion. Three days later, Easter Sunday is the celebration of Jesus's resurrection. This day also marks the end of Lent, a 40-day period of fasting or abstinence. Many Christians celebrate Ascension Day, 40 days after Easter, and especially Pentecost, ten days after the Ascension, when the Apostles were visited by the Holy Spirit.

Easter procession in Tarragona, Spain

Saints and martyrs

Generally speaking, a saint is anyone who shows exceptional devotion and loyalty to Jesus, and lives a life according to his teaching. For Roman Catholics and Orthodox Christians, this necessarily means all those who have died and are now in heaven, although not all of them are recognized as such.

The Roman Catholic Church has a process of canonization, which selects those who deserve official recognition as saints. Protestants also confer the title of saint on particularly venerable figures, but there is no formal procedure. Sainthood may be conferred on a person who has devoted his or her life to the service of others, such as St Francis of Assisi, or to the promotion of the teachings of Jesus, such as the Apostles. Others have literally given their lives in defence of their faith. During periods of persecution, especially in the early Church under Roman rule, many people chose to become martyrs rather than renounce their Christian beliefs, and have since been recognized as saints for their devotion.

The martyrdom of Saint Sebastian, depicted in a Renaissance altarpiece

Christianity in Rome

As the Christian Church evolved, it became a product of the Roman Empire. In the first century, after Jesus's ascension to heaven, the Apostles continued to preach his message in and around Judea. Some of Jesus's disciples travelled more widely, however, and it was Paul the Apostle who took Christianity across the Roman Empire and, with Jesus's closest Apostle Peter, established the early Church in Antioch and in Rome.

Initially, Christianity was barely tolerated by the Roman authorities, and Christians were driven underground by persecution. As increasing numbers of Roman citizens became converts, however, the religion was legalized by the Edict of Milan in 313, and Constantine I became the first Christian emperor. By the end of the fourth century, Christianity had become the Roman state religion. The central authority of the Christian Church gradually shifted from its origins in Jerusalem to Rome, while other cities, such as Alexandria and Constantinople (now Istanbul), became important centres of the faith.

An early Christian fresco from a Roman catacomb

Medievel power

After the fall of Roman Imperial power, the surviving 'Roman Catholic' Church increasingly became a political, as well as religious, power in Europe. Most of the Continent adopted Christianity, which was subject to the central rule of the Pope in Rome. Because it was believed that kings were granted a divine right to rule, the Church exercised considerable influence over the choice of monarchs – so much so that by the time of the establishment of the Holy Roman Empire in 800, it was the Pope who crowned its emperor, Charlemagne.

With a largely illiterate population, the Church also had a monopoly on scholarship and education. In many countries, the Catholic Church's rule was policed by agents of the Sacred Congregation for the Propagation of the Faith, better known as the Inquisition, who censored the publication of books that were considered heretical, and prosecuted people for holding heretical views. The leaders of the Church wielded considerable power throughout the Middle Ages, and were not immune to corruption.

France's soaring Chartres Cathedral is a testament to the power and ambition of the medieval church.

The clergy

As the Christian Church evolved, it developed a leadership structure of clergy who led their congregations in worship and had authority in matters of doctrine. A hierarchy emerged, from the laity – the ordinary members of the church – through the monks and nuns, priests, bishops and cardinals to the overall leader of the Roman Catholic Church, the Pope.

This hierarchy remains little changed in modern Roman Catholicism, and a similar structure exists in the Orthodox Church. Some Protestant denominations, notably Anglicanism, have adopted a similar hierarchy, while others have attempted to return to the more democratic ideals of the early Church. In most Protestant denominations, ordained priests are known as ministers, pastors or parsons. Priesthood was a purely male preserve until the late 20th century, when some of the more liberal branches of Protestantism voted to allow the ordination of women. And, while Catholic priests take vows of celibacy, this is not a requirement in most other branches of Christianity.

Catholicism

With a congregation of over one billion people worldwide, the Catholic Church is the largest denomination in Christianity today. It takes its name from the Greek word *katholikós*, meaning 'universal', and claims to be the one true Christian Church, founded by Jesus and his Apostles. St Peter is believed to have been the first Bishop of Rome, where the headquarters of the Catholic Church, Vatican City, is situated.

Catholicism is distinguished in particular by its emphasis on the seven sacraments: baptism, confirmation, the Eucharist, penance, anointing of the sick, holy orders and holy matrimony. Worship in the Catholic Church is centred on the taking of the Eucharist during the service of Mass. It is a requirement of every Catholic to attend Mass every Sunday and on certain holy days. Another distinguishing feature of Catholicism is a veneration of Mary that is not shared by other denominations, and the belief that she is the Mother of God, a perpetual virgin who was herself conceived without original sin.

The Pope

The head of the Roman Catholic Church is the Bishop of Rome, better known as the Pope (from the Greek word *páppas*, 'father'). Catholics believe that each Pope is the successor of St Peter, whom Jesus entrusted as the 'rock' on which his church would be built. Jesus gave Peter the keys of Heaven; they still feature on the Vatican City's coat of arms.

As the first Bishop of Rome, Peter was assumed to have universal authority over the Christian Church, which passed on to subsequent Popes. Because this authority is God-given, the Pope is believed to be guided by the Holy Spirit and, in matters of faith, doctrine and morality, is considered by Catholics to be infallible. Historically, in addition to his power within the Church, the Pope had considerable influence on rulers and governments. It was not unusual, therefore, for his appointment to be determined for political reasons. In recent times, the Pope has been elected by the College of Cardinals, the highest-ranking clergy of the Roman Catholic Church.

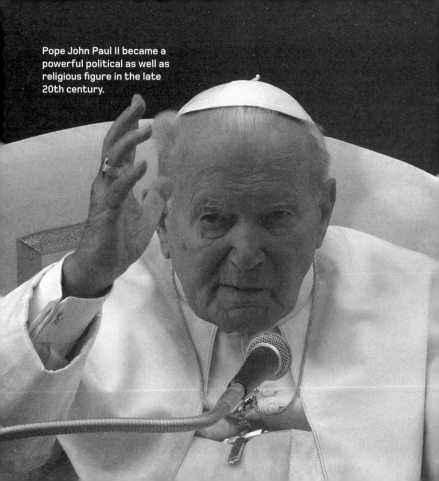

Pope John Paul II became a powerful political as well as religious figure in the late 20th century.

The Great Schism

During the fifth and sixth centuries, the Roman Empire, which stretched across Europe and into the Middle East and Asia, became increasingly divided into western and eastern regions. The mainly Latin-speaking west had its centre in Rome, and was culturally European, while the mainly Greek-speaking east with Constantinople (now Istanbul) as its centre was developing a more oriental culture. The Christian Church was becoming similarly divided, with two diverging traditions emerging.

By the 11th century, matters came to a head, when the Patriarch of Rome, Pope Leo IX, and the Patriarch of Constantinople, Michael Cerularius, clashed over aspects of doctrine and – more significantly – the absolute authority of the Pope over the Church. In 1024, Cerularius was excommunicated from the Catholic Church, marking what became known as the Great Schism. The event created two separate branches of Christianity: the Roman Catholic Church, with the Pope as its absolute leader; and the Eastern Orthodox Church, led by the Patriarch of Constantinople.

The Basilica of Hagia Sophia, once the seat of Eastern Orthodoxy, was converted into a mosque after 1543.

The Orthodox Church

With an estimated 300 million Orthodox Christians, primarily in Greece, Russia, Eastern Europe and the Middle East, the Orthodox Church has its origins in some of the earliest churches established by the Apostles in Jerusalem, Antioch and Alexandria. Its distinctive tradition evolved increasingly independently in the eastern Mediterranean region of the Roman Empire.

As well as developing a somewhat mystical style of worship and Asian-influenced opulence in its architecture and icons, the Orthodox Church adopted a less hierarchical structure than the Church of Rome. It comprises many local self-governing churches, each led by a patriarch, and although the honorary head of the Orthodox Church is the Patriarch of Constantinople, there is no central authority. Bishops are chosen from the monastic orders, and are therefore celibate, but married men are permitted to become priests. Orthodox priests are recognizable by their distinctive robes and headgear, but also because they maintain the Biblical tradition of wearing beards.

The Reformation

The Roman Catholic Church had formidable power in medieval Europe, over both religious and political institutions. Inevitably, that power was abused. The clergy, right up to the Pope, was increasingly seen as being out of touch with ordinary people, but also manipulative and self-serving. There was a growing suspicion of the opulence of the Church, and the exclusivity of its practices, including the services conducted in Latin that meant nothing to a largely illiterate population.

With the invention of the printing press in the 1450s, more people had access to education, and their dissatisfaction with the Church developed into a movement for reform, known as the Reformation. The corruption in the Church was exposed: 'indulgences' (forgiveness for sins) were being sold, as were positions in the clergy. Martin Luther, a 16th-century German priest (opposite) posted a list of '95 Theses' or demands for reform. His excommunication triggered the separation of the protesting (Protestant) churches from the Church of Rome.

Protestantism

Martin Luther's excommunication (see page 286) was the catalyst for a movement that had been stirring for some time in northern Europe. There had been calls for reform in Germany, Switzerland, the Netherlands and Britain. As well as an end to corruption, the reformers favoured a more informed laity, who got their faith from the Bible rather than blindly and superstitiously following tradition. As Luther put it: 'by grace alone through faith alone on the basis of scripture alone.'

While the breakaway Protestants agreed on this aspect of faith, there were many differences of opinion. Rather than a unified Protestant church, their Reformation therefore created a number of different Protestant groups with similar beliefs, among them the Lollards and Hussites (followers of early reformers John Wycliffe and Jan Hus), the Presbyterian movement of John Knox, and the austere Calvinism of John Calvin (opposite). Nevertheless, Protestantism thrived, and today almost 40 per cent of Christians are members of its churches.

Baptists and Methodists

The so-called Age of Enlightenment saw a sea change in attitudes towards the Church in Europe. The authority of Roman Catholicism had been severely dented by the Protestant Reformation (see page 286), and now many people wanted a form of Christianity that suited the rationality of the times.

One such solution was the growing tradition of the Baptist denomination, especially in the US, which rejects the Catholic idea of baptism of infants, and instead advocates baptism for those who can decide for themselves. They also reject the hierarchy of a central Church authority, and allow churches to practise religion as they see fit. Another movement, Methodism, was founded by Anglican minister John Wesley. With its belief that salvation is possible for anyone, and a rejection of the veneration of the clergy, Methodism appealed to the new working class of industrialized society in Britain, and gained a following among slaves in the US. It places great emphasis on doing good works in the community, and evangelizing (see page 300).

The Puritan tradition

The history of Protestantism in England was very different from elsewhere in Europe. Henry VIII's split from the Roman Catholic Church had imposed the new Church of England on the country. Later, in the brief reign of Queen Mary, there was a return to Catholicism. And when Elizabeth I came to the throne, Anglicanism (see page 294) was restored in a revised form. This satisfied neither the Catholics nor the growing number of Puritans, who wanted the Church of England to adopt the austerity of Calvinism.

The Puritans, who objected to the 'popish' ritual, ornaments and pomp of the Anglican Church, enjoyed a brief triumph when Oliver Cromwell defeated the Royalists in the English Civil War, but Anglicanism returned with the Restoration of the monarchy in 1660. A number of dissenting separatist groups established their own reformed churches, including the Society of Friends, or Quakers, founded in the 1650s. Some chose to emigrate, such as the 'Pilgrim Fathers', who fled to Holland and then to America.

Arrival of the Puritans in America,
Antonio Gisbert, 1883

Anglicanism

In England the split from the Roman Catholic Church (see page 292) was more political than religious. Henry VIII (opposite) asked the Pope to annul his marriage to Catherine of Aragon, as she could not give him a male heir, and when this request was turned down, he declared that, as king, he would head the Church in England and separate from the Roman Catholic Church.

The Church of England, or Anglican Church, was created in 1534, on the same principles of reform as Lutheranism and Calvinism. However, it still professed to be a part of the universal, or Catholic, Christian Church. Further reforms came under the leadership of the Archbishop of Canterbury, Thomas Cranmer, including a revised Anglican liturgy and the publication of the Book of Common Prayer. Anglicanism remains the main Christian denomination in England, but is not the only Protestant religion to have emerged in Britain during the Reformation. John Knox, a Scottish colleague of Calvin, founded a prototype of the Presbyterian denomination in Scotland.

Mormons

The Church of Jesus Christ of Latter Day Saints (LDS) is one of many 'breakaway' movements in Christianity claiming to return to the model of the original Church established by the Apostles. It is the largest group within the movement known as Mormonism, after the Book of Mormon, which Joseph Smith Jr claimed was written by the prophet Mormon, as revealed to him by the angel Moroni. The book was written on gold plates, and with God's assistance, Smith translated the quasi-Biblical text.

The narrative tells of the ancient peoples of the Americas, the Nephites and Lamanites, and immigrants from the land of Babel. It also describes an original, true church as Jesus had intended it. The LDS claim to have restored this Church of Christ, but while their teachings are similar to mainstream Christianity in some respects, they are fundamentally different in others (such as a belief that God and humans are manifestations of the same essence). The majority of Mormons are in the US, but the faith also has a following in parts of Central and South America.

Mormon temple in
Salt Lake City, Utah

Dissenting movements

The increasingly liberal, free-thinking society that evolved in the 19th century tolerated dissent from mainstream Christian beliefs, and as a result several breakaway movements formed. Many of these claimed to restore Christianity to its earliest form. Others challenged dogmas that had been taken for granted since the formation of the Church of Rome.

Among the earliest were the Millerites, followers of Baptist preacher William Miller. His argument for the Second Coming of Jesus in 1843 attracted a huge following in America that fragmented when the appointed year passed. Successors included the Seventh-day Adventist Church, which observes Saturday as the Sabbath and awaits an imminent Second Coming. Perhaps the most influential group to emerge, however, was the Jehovah's Witnesses, who consider mainstream Christianity and society to be corrupted by Satan. They reject concepts such as the Holy Trinity and the observance of what they consider to be pagan festivals, and they too anticipate an imminent Armageddon.

Millerite chart predicting the second coming in 1843

Evangelicalism and Revivalism

The 18th century saw a series of 'Great Awakenings' in Protestantism, with the appearance of new and revitalized Christian movements in North America and Britain. The missionary zeal of Methodism in particular inspired enthusiasm for a revival of the Evangelical aspect of Christianity, spreading the word of salvation through faith in Jesus.

Evangelicalism was not a separatist movement, but rather an attitude adopted by Protestant denominations seeking to revitalize their churches with the message of the 'born again' experience. Evangelical Christianity continued to gather momentum through the Revivalist Awakenings of the 19th century and, with the final Great Awakening at the beginning of the 20th century, evolved into Pentecostalism, which emphasizes baptism with the Holy Spirit to experience God as the Apostles had done at Pentecost. A characteristic of Evangelical Revivalist movements is their rejection of solemn piety in favour of a joyous expression of their faith, and a personal experience of God.

Islam

Founded by the prophet Muhammad (*c.* 570– 632 CE) in the early seventh century, Islam quickly became the dominant religion of the Arabic region. Its influence soon spread across Asia and North Africa. Today, almost one-quarter of the world's population are Muslims, and it is considered to be the fastest-growing of all the major religions. There are two main branches of Islam: the majority of Muslims are adherents of Sunni Islam, while Shia Islam accounts for 10 to 20 per cent of believers.

Islam is a strictly monotheistic religion, holding that Allah (God) is transcendent and eternal (the words 'Islam' and 'Muslim' derive from the Arabic words for surrender, peace and security, and carry the religious connotation of submission to God). Like Judaism and Christianity, the religion has its roots in the Abrahamic tradition, and shares many of their prophets. Muslims, however, believe that Muhammad is the last of this line of prophets, to whom Allah revealed his final message, recorded verbatim in the Qur'an, the Islamic holy scripture.

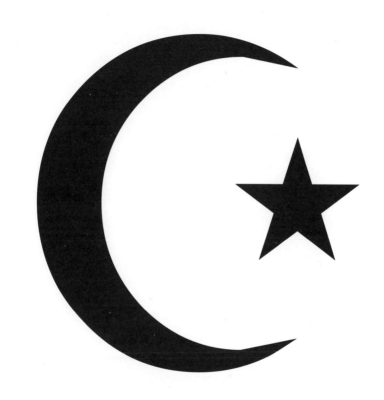

The prophets

Central to Islamic belief is the testament of a line of prophets, considered by Muslims to be the messengers of Allah. Figures that feature in the scriptures of both Judaism and Christianity – Adam, Noah, Abraham, Moses and Ishmael – are recognized as prophets who taught the core message of Islam, submission to God. Also included is Jesus, but he, along with the others, is seen as a human prophet rather than divine.

According to Islamic belief, the message brought by these prophets was the authentic faith of Islam. This later became corrupted by various interpretations, and Allah chose the Prophet Muhammad as His final messenger. Through the angel Jibril (Gabriel), he dictated what was to be regarded as the Final Testament, in the form of the Qur'an, and entrusted Muhammad with the task of taking this divine message to the whole world. Muslims regard Muhammad as the last of God's prophets, and as a mark of respect normally follow his name in speech and writing with the words 'peace and blessings be upon him'.

The name of the Prophet Muhammad combined with an Islamic *salat* prayer in elaborate Arabic calligraphy.

Muhammad

The Prophet Muhammad was born in Mecca *c.* 570, a time
when Arabia was divided into many tribes following a variety
of traditional polytheistic religions. Orphaned at an early
age, he was brought up by his uncle Abu Talib, and became a
merchant in the city of Mecca. As a young man, he became
increasingly preoccupied with religion, and frequently sought
retreat in the surrounding mountains. It was during one of
these retreats that he later reported that he had been visited
by the angel Jibril, who brought him revelations from Allah.

Muhammad built up a following in Mecca, but the local tribes
were antagonistic and he was forced to flee to Medina in
622 – a migration known as the Hijra, which is taken as the
beginning of the Islamic calendar. Muhammad united the people
of Medina under his political as well as religious leadership. He
also amassed a large army, which took the city of Mecca without
significant resistance In 629. By the time of his death, in 632,
Muhammad's Islamic rule had spread across almost all of Arabia.

According to legend, the Quba Mosque at Medina was founded by Muhammad himself.

The Islamic Empire

Muhammad proved an effective military and political leader. Having united several disparate Arabian tribes under Islam, he established a form of government with the so-called Constitution of Medina (c. 622 CE) and led an army of followers to Mecca. From there, he brought most of the Arabian peninsula into a single polity, and laid the foundations of an Islamic empire.

His political and spiritual heirs, known as caliphs, continued to expand the influence of Islam in a succession of caliphates (Rashidun, Umayyad, Abbasid, Fatimid, Ayyubid, Mamluk and Ottoman), ruling territory that stretched from the Middle East over North Africa and the Iberian peninsula, and across Asia into India. With the fall of the Ottoman Empire afer 1918, new nation-states emerged, and enthusiasm for a supranational caliphate waned. These new countries generally retained a distinctly Islamic influence. Some are ruled by royal families, others by secular governments; some with Islam as an official or state religion, or even, as in present-day Iran, under theocratic rule.

Since 1979, Iran has been ruled by a council of 88 Islamic theologians known as the Assembly of Experts.

The Islamic Golden Age

The caliphates that ruled the Islamic world after Muhammad's death brought prosperity to the Middle East, and a Golden Age of scientific and cultural achievements that lasted from the 8th century until the Mongol invasions of the 13th century.

From the time of the Caliph Harun al-Rashid (r.786–809), Islam actively encouraged philosophy and scientific investigation. Scholarship was highly prized, and institutions such as the Bayt al-Hikma (House of Wisdom) in Baghdad were established as centres of learning and research. Alongside Islamic theology and law, scholars studied Greek and Roman philosophy, preserving and translating many important texts. They made significant contributions to the understanding of science, including advances in astronomy, mathematics, medicine, chemistry and engineering that laid foundations for the later Scientific Revolution in Europe. Alongside academic disciplines, the caliphate also fostered a flourishing of culture, and some of the finest Islamic art, architecture and poetry dates from this time.

A monument to the influential 9th-century Persian mathematician, astronomer and geographer al-Khwarizmi in Khiva, Uzbekistan.

The Qur'an

The holy book of Islam, the Qur'an, is a record of revelations made by the angel Jibril to Muhammad between 609 and his death in 632. Muslims believe that the Qur'an, meaning 'recitation', is the word of Allah, dictated verbatim to the Prophet. The Qur'an did not appear in book form during Muhammad's lifetime, but was memorized and passed on orally. Only some of the verses were written down by his followers, among them his cousin Ali ibn Abi Talib. The complete Qur'an was compiled from these memorized verses and written fragments shortly after Muhammad's death.

Written in an elegant poetic prose considered the epitome of Arabic literature, the Qur'an takes the form of 114 sections known as *suras*, each one comprising a number of verses known as *ayat*. The majority of the *suras* date from Muhammad's time in Mecca, with an additional 24 from the period following his migration to Medina. Much of the text presents a fresh interpretation of previous Biblical narrative, and, in its commentary, offers moral and spiritual guidance.

Muslims commonly use *Misbaha* prayer beads to count prayers while reading the Qur'an.

Paradise and Hell

Throughout the Qur'an there are references to both the afterlife and the Last Day. Muslims believe that, after death, they remain in their graves until Yawm al-Qiyamah, the Day of Resurrection. They will then be judged on the deeds of their earthly life and sent either to Jannah (Paradise) or Jahannam (Hell). Muslims are instructed to prepare for this imminent day of judgement, also known in the Qur'an simply as The Hour, which will be heralded by a mighty noise, followed by a cataclysm and the resurrection of all the dead.

Those who prove themselves good Muslims will be transported to Paradise, described as a garden in which they will receive everything that they have yearned for in their earthly lives. Unbelievers, heretics, apostates and sinners will be sentenced to spend an eternity of spiritual and physical suffering in one of seven increasingly punitive levels of Hell. Those considered enemies of Islam do not have to wait until Yawm al-QiyĐmah, but are condemned to Hell from the moment of their death.

Hadith

While the Qur'an is revered in Islam as the word of Allah, it is not the only book offering spiritual guidance. There are also collections of the teachings of Muhammad and accounts of his deeds and character, each known as a *Hadith*, meaning 'report' or 'narrative'. These collections supplement the teaching of the Qur'an. They present a comprehensive account of the life of Muhammad – the *Sunna* (trodden path) – which is held to be the example all Muslims should follow.

The *Hadith* collections originate mainly from contemporary oral sources, and were compiled over the course of the eighth and ninth centuries, 100 years or more after Muhammad's death. As a result, Muslim scholars often disagree over the authenticity of some of the texts.

Several different collections of *Hadiths* have been compiled, such as the Six Books that form the canon of the Sunni branch of Islam, and the Four Books of the Shia canon.

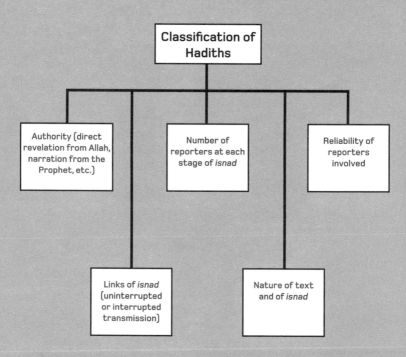

Classification of Hadiths

- Authority (direct revelation from Allah, narration from the Prophet, etc.)
- Number of reporters at each stage of *isnad*
- Reliability of reporters involved
- Links of *isnad* (uninterrupted or interrupted transmission)
- Nature of text and of *isnad*

Hadith are classified in a sophisticated system that takes account of both their content, and the chain of reporters (*isnad*) involved prior to their being collected and written down.

Five Pillars of Islam

According to a *Hadith* recounted by Muhammad's brother-in-law, Abdallah ibn Umar, the Prophet stated that Islam is based on five core principles, often referred to as the 'Five Pillars of Islam'. These are: *shahada*, profession of faith; *salat*, prayer; *zakat*, almsgiving; *sawm*, fasting; and *hajj*, pilgrimage to Mecca.

Although many do not consider them comprehensive, these five simple principles encapsulate the essential elements of the belief and its practice, and what Muhammad described as a small burden of requirements from every Muslim. The five pillars are accepted and practised by all followers of Islam. Some branches – especially of Shia Islam – have extended the list to include other practices, and in some cases modified their meaning somewhat. Twelver Shia, for example, does not include *shahada*, as this is considered the foundation upon which all other principles are based. Instead, it proposes five principles of belief, the Usul al-Din, and ten practices, the Furu' al-Din (Ancillaries of the Faith).

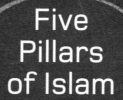

Five
Pillars
of Islam

Shahada

Salat

Zakat

Sawm

Hajj

No god but Allah

The first and central of the Five Pillars of Islam is *shahada* (testimony or witness), a two-part profession of faith generally translated into English as '(I testify that) there is no god but Allah and Muhammad is the messenger of God'. Firstly, it affirms belief in *tawhid*, the monotheistic principle of the oneness of God. In Arabic, God is known as Allah, from *al-ilah* or *allah* meaning 'the God', reinforcing the idea that He is the one and only true God. Also included in the *shahada* is the acknowledgement of the authority of Muhammad as the final and true Prophet, relaying His message to the world.

In order to become a Muslim, a person must make this simple declaration of faith. The *shahada* is traditionally whispered into the ear of every newborn Muslim baby, as well as into the ear of the recently deceased. Muslims are expected constantly to reaffirm their belief, too, and recite the *shahada* several times a day, every day, particularly at the regular call to prayer (see page 322).

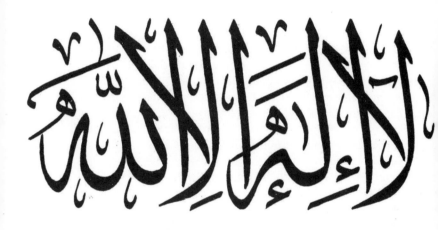

Calligraphic representation of the first *shahada*: 'There is no god but Allah'.

Call to prayer

The second of the Five Pillars of Islam, *salat*, is translated as 'prayer', but in practice refers to all aspects of the act of worship required of every Muslim five times a day. The faithful are traditionally called to prayer by a muezzin from the minaret of a mosque at dawn, noon, mid-afternoon, dusk and evening. Muslims are obliged to purify themselves by washing, and then perform the prescribed actions and prayers while facing the *qibla* – the direction of Mecca.

The *salat* begins with the affirmation 'God is great', and is normally followed by recitation of prayers including the *shahada* and the opening passage of the Qur'an. The prayers are offered from a kneeling position, and accompanied by raising and lowering the hands in low bows and prostrating. The *salat* can be done anywhere at the appropriate time of day, on a special prayer mat. The fact that Muslims all worship at the same time of day – performing the same rituals and facing Mecca – is symbolic of the unity of their faith.

Almsgiving

Much emphasis is placed on social responsibility in Islam. It is considered to be a religious duty to help those in need and this is enshrined in the principle of *zakat*, the third of the Five Pillars of Islam.

All adult Muslims are not only expected to perform acts of charity, but are also required to give a proportion of their income in alms. This is seen as a type of tax, based on both income and assets, and traditionally takes the form of one-fortieth (2.5 per cent) of a person's wealth above an agreed minimum.

The money is then distributed to the poor and disadvantaged, but also to the clergy to pay for their services in spreading the word of Islam. Although this is generally given voluntarily, as an obligation and observance of the faith, in some countries it is officially collected as a tax by the government. In addition to *zakat*, some branches of the faith also require a donation of 20 per cent of profits from business, industrial assets or windfalls.

Ramadan

Fasting is the fourth of the Five Pillars of Islam, and is considered a means of spiritual purification, as well as a means of instilling in Muslims the virtues of self-control and obedience, and an awareness of the plight of the needy.

The most important period of fasting is during Ramadan – the ninth month of the Islamic lunar calendar – the penultimate day of which is celebrated as the anniversary of Muhammad's first encounter with Jibril. For the whole of this month, all Muslims who are physically able are obliged to refrain from eating, drinking, sexual activity and smoking from sunrise to sunset, and to spend the day in contemplation and devotion, including reciting a prayer only used during Ramadan. Most families gather for a pre-dawn meal to prepare themselves for each day of fasting, and again after sunset for a more celebratory supper. At the end of Ramadan, marked by the sighting of the crescent new moon, the end of fasting is celebrated in the feast of Eid al-Fitr, a highpoint in the Islamic year.

During Ramadan:

✗ No eating or drinking from dawn to sunset
✗ Lower your gaze and guard your modesty
✗ No arguing or fighting
✗ No swearing or lying
✗ No smoking
✗ No wasting of time
✗ No music

✓ Pray five times a day
✓ Study Islamic knowledge
✓ Learn and recite the Qur'an
✓ Recite the names of God
✓ Make supplications to Allah
✓ Give to charity

The hajj

The last of the Five Pillars of Islam is the *hajj* – a pilgrimage to the holy city of Mecca in Saudi Arabia. At least once in their lifetime, all Muslims are expected to perform this religious duty if they are physically able and can afford to do so.

Each year, from 8-12 Dhu al-Hijjah (the last month of the Islamic calendar), pilgrims arrive in Mecca and make their way to al-Masjid al-Haram (the Grand Mosque), the most holy Islamic site. At its centre is the Kaaba, a cube-shaped structure believed to have been built by Ibrahim (Abraham). This site of pilgrimage for thousands of years is now the focus of the *qibla*, the direction of Islamic prayer. Following a ceremonial purification, pilgrims walk seven times anticlockwise around the Kaaba, and during the next week may take part in other rituals, such as drinking from the Well of Zamzam, symbolically stoning the devil by throwing stones at three pillars and visiting the burial place of Muhammad in Medina. The end of the period is marked by the three-day festival of Eid al-Adha.

Crowds worship at the Kaaba in Mecca.

The mosque

At the centre of any Islamic community is the mosque, the building in which Muslims gather to pray, especially on Friday, the Day of Assembly. But a mosque is more than a place of worship, providing a social as well as a spiritual focus.

The heart of every mosque is the *musalla* (prayer hall), with a *qibla* wall opposite its entrance indicating the direction of prayer towards Mecca. Many mosques also have other rooms, colonnades and courtyards to provide spaces for study and social interaction, both essential aspects of Islamic culture.

Many early mosques were built in the flat-roofed, columnar style known as hypostyle, which offered cool and shady arcades for contemplation and study, as well as a courtyard to cope with the large congregations at Friday prayers. Some had a minaret from which the faithful could be called to prayer. During the Ottoman Empire, a new style emerged featuring Byzantine-inspired domes, such as the magnificent Blue Mosque in Istanbul.

Fourteenth-century al-Nasir Muhammad Mosque, Cairo

Islamic clergy

In Sunni Islam, the largest branch of the faith, the leaders of the mosque are seen as officials chosen for their scholarship, rather than as divinely appointed intermediaries between Allah and the congregation. There are three main positions: *mu'adhdhin* (muezzin), who calls to prayer; *khatib* (preacher); and imam, who leads the prayer. The imam is also a community leader with pastoral responsibilities as well as offering guidance in religious matters. Other officials attached to a mosque include teachers and scholars of Islamic theology and law.

Imams in the minority Shia Islam have a very different status. Shi'a Muslims believe that Allah authorizes a line of succession through Muhammad, the Ahl al-Bayt, and that He chooses the imams to be the leaders of Shia communities. Because of their divine appointment, these Shia imams are considered infallible, and to have both divine authority and knowledge. In the last hundred years in Shia Islam, the title of Ayatollah has become used for the highest-ranking Islamic scholar-officials.

Sharia

The Qur'an provides more than religious and moral guidance. It has an influence on every aspect of a Muslim's life according to the principles of sharia, the Islamic legal system.

Sharia is the law set out by Allah, as opposed to the secular legislation decided by governments and courts. The primary source of sharia is the Qur'an, the word of God, which lays down many of the fundamental moral, religious and legal rules of Islam. Certain aspects are also derived from the *Hadith* (see page 316).

The law is administered by various sharia councils, who adjudicate on matters ranging from crime and civil disputes to contracts and marriages, politics and economics, and issues of personal morality and religious observance. Judgements can sometimes be made by direct reference to a statement made by Allah in the Qur'an. Where the ruling is not clear, the judgement is based on interpretations of the Qur'an and *Hadith*, made by scholars of Islamic law, whose opinions are known as fatwas.

Islamic scholars confer prior to delivering a sharia judgement at a court in Katsina, northern Nigeria.

Jihad

Jihad, the religious duty of all Muslims to defend the faith, is an essential element of Islam. The Arabic *jihad* means 'striving' or 'struggle', and refers to both an inner struggle – the greater jihad – against evil in oneself and striving to live as a good Muslim, and the outward struggle – the lesser jihad – against the enemies of Islam.

There is, however, no universally agreed definition of jihad, even among Muslims, and the concept has become increasingly controversial with its use in association with armed conflict and terrorism. Islamic scholars generally agree with the principle of personal jihad (the inner spiritual quest), but there are differences of opinion as to the extent that jihad permits military action or other forms of physical violence. Islam, in general, preaches peace and tolerance, but Muhammad, who himself led an army against infidels in Mecca, said that physical force is sometimes necessary to defend Islam against its enemies.

Halal food and drink

Muslims are expected to adhere to comprehensive guidance when it comes to what is either permitted or forbidden in everyday life. All objects and actions are categorized as either *fard* (obligatory), *mustahabb* (recommended), *halal* (permitted), *makruh* (disapproved) or *haram* (forbidden) by Islamic law.

The term *halal* is most frequently associated with food. It refers to both permitted foods and their preparation, although generally speaking, unless a foodstuff is specifically designated *haram* (for instance, blood and intoxicants such as alcohol) it is permitted. However, the concept also extends to items produced using non-*halal* practices, and non-food items such as medicines or cosmetics containing *haram* ingredients.

Laws governing meat are especially strict: animals must be slaughtered by a Muslim in the name of Allah, by cutting its throat with one deep incision while holding its head in the direction of Mecca, and then allowing the blood to drain from the body.

Women and Islam

The status of women in Islam has been been a focus of much debate in recent years, with the rise of feminism and women's rights. While Islamic scholars maintain that the Qur'an states that men and women are equal in the eyes of Islam, some sharia rulings offer women lesser rights than men in matters of marriage, property and education.

The question of women's dress has been particularly, controversial, especially in Western countries with significant Muslim populations, where it is associated with oppression. A common perception is that Islam obliges women to wear such items of clothing as the *hijab* (head covering), *niqab* (veil) or *burka* (full-body covering), but this is more a matter of local practice than Islamic requirement. These modes of dress are not prescribed in the Qur'an or *Hadith*, which state merely that both men and women should dress modestly and, more specifically, that women should not display their beauty outside of the family. Interpretations of this guidance differ from society to society.

Art and architecture

In the so-called Golden Age of Islam (see page 310), the arts flourished throughout the Muslim world. In particular, Islamic styles of art and architecture emerged, influenced by the teachings of the religion and its encouragement of scholarship.

Islamic art was, and remains, almost invariably abstract. Unlike most other religions, there are very few portrayals of God, which are regarded as a form of idolatry (representations of Muhammad and the prophets only appear in early Islamic art). Instead, religious art has been reserved for the decoration of mosques, and the illumination of the calligraphy in the Qur'an. Mosques, especially of this period, are adorned with repetitive patterns of floral and geometric figures, in lavish mediums such as mosaic, or quotations from verses of the Qur'an in artistic calligraphy. Similarly, the architecture of the mosques themselves is generally highly geometrically ordered, and features rows of repeating columns and arches, or symmetrically placed towers and domes around a central dome.

Sunni and Shia

Following Muhammad's death, his followers were divided as to who should be his successor. One of his closest disciples, Umar ibn al-Khattab, nominated Muhammad's father-in-law Abu Bakr, who was then elected as the first caliph. But some Muslims disputed his claim to the caliphate, believing the Prophet had nominated his cousin and son-in-law, Ali ibn Abi Talib, to succeed. This disagreement led to the separation of the two main branches of Islam: 'Sunni' supporters of Abu Bakr, which today accounts for around 85 per cent of all Muslims; and 'Shia' supporters of Ali, forming the bulk of the population in Iran, Iraq, Azerbaijan and Bahrain, and substantial minorities elsewhere.

While Sunnis recognize the legitimacy of Abu Bakr and the first caliphs, Shias believe that only members of Ahl al-Bayt, the family of the Prophet, can be Muhammad's heirs. Disagreement as to the legitimacy of the imams after Ali led to further subdivision of Shia Islam into Fivers, Seveners and Twelvers (the largest group in Shia), according to the number of prophets they recognize.

Modern distribution of Sunni and Shia Muslims

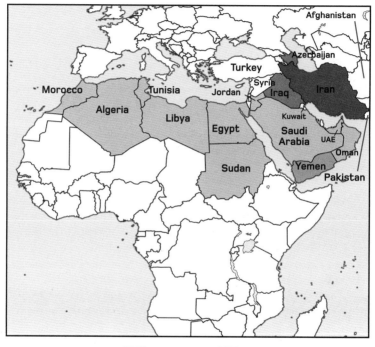

Shia population:

< 10%

10–25%

25–50%

> 50%

Sufism

In the 12th and 13th centuries, a new, more mystical, branch of Islam emerged among Muslims seeking a direct personal experience of God. The practice, Sufism, promoted living an ascetic lifestyle known as *fanaa*, renouncing the material world and purifying the body and soul. Adherents, sometimes known as dervishes, or fakirs, practise fasting, celibacy and *dhikr*, the repetition of the names of God.

There are several orders of Sufism, probably the best known being the Mevlevi, founded by the mystic poet Jalal al-Din Rumi (1207–73) in Turkey. Rumi advocated the use of music and dance, such as the meditative spinning dance of the whirling dervishes, to induce an ecstatic state in which to experience God. Music in worship was, and still is, frowned upon by most other branches of Islam, and even forbidden by some, and mysticism was similarly seen as heretical. As a result, Sufis have often faced persecution by other branches of Islam, and the practice has been banned in some Muslim countries.

Conservative and Fundamentalist Islam

By the beginning of the 20th century, the political influence of Islam was on the wane. The Mogul Empire had disappeared, the Ottoman Empire was in decline, and Western countries had colonized much of the world. Some Muslims felt that the religious values of Islam had been eroded, and called for a return to fundamental Islamic ideals. The revivalist movement centred initially on the activism of Sayyib Qutb in Egypt, who advocated a rejection of Westernization, and a renewal of the idea of jihad.

More recently, the rejection of Western modernization and secularization has been adopted by followers of 18th-century scholar, Muhammad ibn Abd al-Wahhab, who sought strict adherence to sharia (see page 334), especially in orthodox Islamic countries such as Saudi Arabia. The notion of jihad as a religious duty, not only to defend Islam, but also to defeat its enemies, has been taken up by some extreme Wahhabi groups, and has inspired the rise of Islamist terrorist organizations such as al-Qaeda, Boko Haram and the so-called Islamic State (IS).

Members of a fundamentalist Muslim group in Kano State, Nigeria

The spread of Islam

Islam became established in many places through Islamic imperialism, as the caliphates extended their territories from Arabia into Asia and Africa (see page 308). But its influence was not only spread by colonization. The religion was taken up in some countries through contact with Muslim traders, especially in sub-Saharan Africa and Indonesia, where it remains the majority religion to the present day.

Islam has also gained a following in many countries through the migration of Muslims across the world. For example, the Nation of Islam movement in the United States, loosely based on Sunni Islam, was founded by Wallace Fard Muhammad in 1930 to provide a spiritual focus for descendants of African slaves.

Today, Islam is the second largest religion in the world, and 57 states, members of the supranational Organization of Islamic Cooperation (OIC), identify themselves as Muslim-majority countries, or at least with a large Muslim population.

Influential preacher Elijah Muhammad addresses a crowd including boxer Muhammad Ali (centre far left).

Sikhism

Sikhism is the youngest of the major religions and, with more than 25 million followers, is the world's fifth largest. It originated in the Punjab region of present-day Pakistan c. 1500, amid increasing conflict between the indigenous Hindu population and Muslim invaders. It became established at much the same time as the Islamic Mogul Empire in India.

The religion is based on the teachings of Guru Nanak, who rejected both the polytheism of Hinduism and the exclusivity of Islam. Instead, he preached faith in Ik Onkar (the One Supreme Creator), a spirit accessible to people of all religions. To make a connection with this timeless, formless spirit in order to achieve enlightenment, Guru Nanak advocated meditation and living a virtuous, selfless life of service. In this respect, Sikhism has similarities with Hinduism and Buddhism. However, it has a stronger emphasis on social justice, as Sikhs believe all humanity to be equal and deserving of respect, regardless of religion, and that it is a religious and moral duty to strive for their benefit.

Guru Nanak

The founder of the Sikh religion, Nanak (1469–1539), was born in the village of Talwandi (now Nankana Sahib in his honour) in what is now Pakistan. His family was Hindu, and as a young man he showed a fascination for spiritual matters, often meditating quietly alone.

According to Sikh tradition, at the age of about 30, Nanak had a revelation while bathing in the river. He said that he experienced the call of God, who offered him a cup of *amrit* (nectar), with the words: 'This is the cup of the adoration of God's name ... Go, rejoice of my name and teach others to do so. I have bestowed the gift of my name upon you. Let this be your vocation.' When he returned home, Nanak explained that he now realized 'there is neither Hindu nor Muslim, but only man ... God is neither Hindu nor Muslim and the path that I follow is God's.' He devoted his life to preaching, earning himself the title 'guru' (teacher), and his followers became know as Sikhs, derived from the Sanskrit word for student or disciple.

Guru Granth Sahib

Following the death of Guru Nanak in 1539, leadership of the Sikh religion passed to a succession of gurus in an unbroken line until 1708. The 10th of these, Guru Gobind Singh (1666–1708), declared that he was to be the last of the human gurus, and nominated as his successor the holy scriptures of Sikhism, to be known as the Guru Granth Sahib (the sanskrit *granth*, means 'book'). This, he said, was to be the final, eternal living guru, embodying the wisdom of all the previous gurus.

The work compiles many compositions by the gurus and other Sikh scholars, and consists of 1,430 pages of hymns and prayers written in a poetic style associated with the ragas of north Indian classical music. Readings from the Guru Granth Sahib are central to Sikh worship, and each *gurdwara* (Sikh temple) has a copy of it, often lavishly decorated. The book is treated with great reverence, and in *gurdwaras* it is respectfully sited on a 'throne', protected with embroidered cloths, in the custody of a temple official known as a *granthi*.

Path to salvation

Sikhism offers guidance for its followers on the correct way of living, or dharma, that provides a path to salvation (see page 90). For the Sikh, the ultimate goal is freedom from rebirth, which is the last of five stages of the spiritual journey.

The first stage is that of being a wrong-doer, which can be overcome by renouncing the five vices (see page 360) and living a selfless life. The second is a state of devotion to God and the teachings of the gurus. The third stage is the shedding of ego and achieving a spiritual union with *akaal*, the eternal and timeless spirit of the One Supreme Creator. This comes, not only from meditation and prayer, but also by actively living a useful life. The fourth stage is a state of eternal bliss, while the fifth and final step is a complete liberation from the cycle of rebirth. Although the Universe is subject to the laws of karma (see page 96), Sikhs believe that humans have been shown God's grace by the fact that they have been given life, and this grace will also help their progress on the road to salvation.

Liberation from rebirth

Eternal bliss

Spiritual union with
akaal

Devotion to God and study
of the gurus

Wrong-doing

Five vices

The main obstacle a Sikh faces on the journey to oneness with God and freedom from rebirth is *maya*, which means something akin to 'unreality', and embodies the idea of the illusory quality of material worth. This is not because the world itself is deceptive, but results from a human failing in valuing the material life – and sensual gratification – higher than spiritual values.

This is the error frequently made by Sikhs embarking on the first stage of the path to salvation (see page 358) – not necessarily sinning, but living life in the wrong way. *Maya* offers several worldly temptations that distract us from the true path, but deliver only temporary satisfaction and pleasure. Sikhs identify five of these vices, often referred to as the 'five thieves', as follows: *ahankaar* (ego), *kaam* (lust), *krodth* (anger), *lobh* (greed) and *moh* (pride or attachment). Sikhs believe that the ills of the world – and, in particular, the modern world – can be attributed to the influence of *maya*, and our preoccupation with material goods and pleasure-seeking.

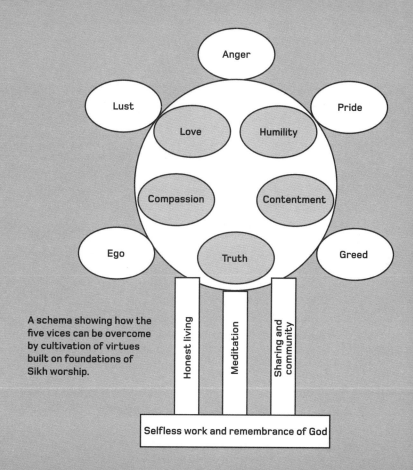

Anger

Lust

Pride

Love

Humility

Compassion

Contentment

Ego

Truth

Greed

Honest living

Meditation

Sharing and community

A schema showing how the five vices can be overcome by cultivation of virtues built on foundations of Sikh worship.

Selfless work and remembrance of God

The Khalsa

During the period of the first ten gurus, Sikhs were regarded as heretics by both the indigenous Hindus and their Muslims rulers, and often suffered persecution. In response, the last human guru, Gobind Singh, created an order of baptized Sikhs who would defend the faith and protect the oppressed and weak. These are the Khalsa (the Pure), who pledge to uphold the core values of the Sikh religion by leading a saintly life, while at the same time having the courage of a lion and being prepared to act as a warrior when necessary – the qualities of the Sant-Sipahi, or saint soldier.

In a ceremony of initiation known as *amrit sanchar*, the 'nectar ritual', prospective Khalsa drink sweetened water symbolizing the nectar that God offered to Guru Nanak (see page 354) and make their vows. Once baptized as members of the Khalsa, Sikhs are known as Amritdhari, those who have drunk nectar, and male initiates are given the surname Singh, meaning 'lion', while female initiates are called Kaur, 'princess'.

The five Ks

One of the commitments made during initiation into the Khalsa (see page 362) is to wear the five articles of faith, known as the 'five Ks'. These are outward signs of the vows taken at baptism, each with its own symbolic significance.

The first is *kesh* (uncut hair). Hair is considered a gift from God, and *kesh* symbolizes acceptance of God's will, by not interfering with His intentions. Men often wear a turban as a practical way of dealing with long hair and, while the turban is not one of the articles of faith, it is probably the most widely recognized sign of Sikhism. The *kangha*, a small wooden comb, symbolizes personal cleanliness, and is used for grooming twice a day. The *kara*, a metal bracelet, signifies allegiance to God and is used as a reminder to renounce the five vices (see page 360). The *kachera*, loose cotton underwear, is worn as a symbol of chastity and a reminder to refrain from desire and attachment. Finally, the *kirpan* is a small ceremonial sword, a sign of the saint-soldier's duty to resist evil and protect the weak, and is only to be used defensively.

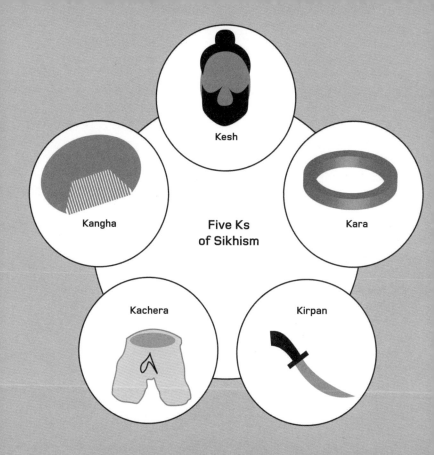

Sikh worship

The Sikh religion places great stress on being both inclusive and egalitarian. This stems from the founder Guru Nanak's rejection of the conflict between Islam and Hinduism, and of the injustices of the Hindu class system.

Sikhs believe that all humans, regardless of class, race, gender or even religion, are equal under the one God, and that no religion has an exclusive claim on the absolute truth. Because of this, there is no separate class of clergy or priests in Sikhism, and the act of worship can be performed by anyone and in any place. The Guru Granth Sahib, the holy scripture, is likewise available to all; during worship, recitations from the sacred text can be made by any adult, male or female. Sikhs are expected to show their devotion by private meditation on the name of God, rather than elaborate ritual or ceremony. Morning and evening prayer services are simple, and consist of singing passages from the Guru Granth Sahib. Sikhs celebrate several festivals during the year, mostly commemorating events in the lives of the gurus.

Sikhs celebrate the festival of Hola Mohalla

The gurdwara

Meaning the 'gateway to the guru' or 'house of the guru', the *gurdwara* is more than simply a place of worship for Sikhs. As well as fulfilling its primary function as a *harmandir* (temple), it also plays an important role as a social centre for the Sikh community.

Traditionally, a *gurdwara* has four doors, all of them always open to anyone and each with its own significance: the door of peace; the door of livelihood; the door of learning; and the door of grace. Within the *gurdwara*, the Guru Granth Sahib is kept in a prominent place and is central to acts of worship.

The building offers space for education, cultural activities and pastoral care. And, in keeping with the core Sikh philosophy of service to others, it offers hospitality to all. Those in need can find protection and shelter, and each *gurdwara* has a kitchen that provides *langar* (free food) for the congregation and any visitors, who sit on the floor to eat communally.

The Sikh Golden Temple at Amritsar

Gnosticism

The 19th century saw a plethora of new religious movements emerge around the world – some of them breakaway sects of existing faiths, and others with much more divergent beliefs connected to ancient or folk religions. Among them was a revival of the ancient Hellenistic belief in Gnosticism, which had arisen at much the same time as the early Christian Church.

Several Gnostic movements emerged in Europe, incorporating elements of the Abrahamic religions and focusing on the idea that gnosis (knowledge) is the key to understanding God and achieving a spiritual liberation from the material world. The world was created, they say, not by God, but by a lesser supernatural spirit. The true nature of the good and perfect God is hidden from this flawed world, except for those who can discover the esoteric gnosis. This knowledge is variously thought to be encoded in the mythology of ancient religions, in Buddhist philosophy, and even in the teachings of Jesus, who some believe to be a divine messenger sent to reveal the secrets of gnosis.

Theosophy

The late-19th-century Theosophical movement sought knowledge of the nature of divinity and an understanding of the mysteries of the Universe, and believed that this knowledge could be discovered by philosophical investigation. Theosophy (from the Greek for 'God's wisdom', and an explicit reference to philosophy) also shifted the emphasis from mystical beliefs in hidden knowledge, available only to the initiated, to a more rational and even scientific quest for knowledge.

The combination of religious and philosophical enquiry gave the movement a degree of respectability, and the Theosophical Society, founded in New York in 1875, quickly gained a following among the world's literati. Helena Blavatsky, one of its founding members (opposite), became a household name for her books on mystical philosophy and religion. Her brand of Theosophy emphasized the foundation of a universal brotherhood and the study of comparative religion. Following her death in 1891, the movement fragmented into several successor organizations.

Spiritualism

In Victorian Britain, and throughout the English-speaking world, there was a fascination with the idea of communicating with the dead. Seances were fashionable and mediums – equivalents of traditional shamans (see page 32) – became celebrities. Alongside this populist interest, there was a more serious-minded Spiritualist movement, which established churches in the UK and the US from the mid-19th century onwards.

Spiritualists believe in an 'infinite intelligence' rather than a God, and that the Universe and everything in it is an expression of this. Part of that Universe is humankind, and each of us has an immortal soul that lives on after our physical death, and continues to grow spiritually. It is possible for us to make contact with these spirits in the afterlife, and learn from their experience. A similar movement, known as Spiritism, developed in mainland Europe, and later spread to South America and French Indochina. Inspired by the scientific investigations carried out by the Frenchman Allan Kardec, it placed more emphasis on reincarnation.

New pagans

Disillusionment with the conservatism of mainstream religions and the lack of spirituality of the scientific world prompted a revival of pre-Christian religions in the 20th century. Collectively known as Neopaganism, these include reconstructions of the ancient English and Celtic religions, Wicca and Druidism.

Neopagan religions are generally pantheistic, placing emphasis on the sacredness of the natural world. As little is known of the actual beliefs and practices of the original religions, both Wicca and Druidism draw heavily on Victorian descriptions. Modern Wicca originated with followers of Gerald Gardner in 1940s' Britain, and influenced a number of different interpretations of the core beliefs of a Universe divided into earthly and magic planes, and a complementary God and Goddess signifying the duality of the world. Druidism, reinstituted as a cultural movement as early as the 18th century, also saw a revival of interest in its spiritual aspects, as an initially monotheistic philosophy compatible with Christianity was transformed into a polytheistic, neopagan belief system.

Japanese New Religions

Such has been the importance of new religious movements in Japan since the mid-19th century that the word Shinshukyo (Japanese New Religions) was coined to describe them.

Perhaps the first distinct new religion was Tenrikyo, founded by Miki Nakayama in 1838 following a revelation from God during a Buddhist ritual. In Tenrikyo, Tenri-O-no-Mikoto (God the Parent) encourages followers to pursue the 'joyous life' of service and charity towards other people, brushing away the mental 'dust' of egotism. Other 19th-century Shinshukyo include Konkokyo (founded in 1859) and Oomoto (founded in 1892), in effect modern sects of Shinto; and Soka Gakkai (founded in 1930), based on the teachings of the 13th-century Japanese Buddhist priest Nichiren. Among the more modern Shinshukyo are some that are considered cults, such as the controversial Happy Science, whose founder Ryuho Okawa claims to be the divine El Cantare, an embodiment of religious figures including Buddha, Christ, Muhammad and Confucius.

Crest of Konkokyo

Falun Gong

Following the establishment of The People's Republic of China (1949), and the subsequent Cultural Revolution of the 1960s, religion of all kinds was suppressed in the country. The ban on religion was relaxed after the death of Mao Zedong, allowing people to follow traditional beliefs, but also to form new ones. Among these was Falun Gong, which amalgamated several strands of ancient and modern Chinese thought.

Falun Gong emerged from the martial-arts exercise qigong, which had become popular as physical training in the early years of the communist era, and with increasing tolerance of religion in the 1980s began to incorporate elements of Daoism, Confucianism and Buddhism. The physical exercise is, like yoga, an aid to meditation in the Buddhist way, as well as a cultivation of body, mind and spirit. Translating as 'law wheel practice', the art also entails a moral philosophy based on the traditional Chinese virtues of *zhen* (truthfulness), *shàn* (benevolence), and *ren* (forbearance).

Key Falun Gong exercises

Falun Heavenly Circulation

Strengthening Divine Powers

Buddha Showing a Thousand Hands

Falun Standing Stance

Penetrating the Two Cosmic Extremes

Bahá'í

The founder of the Bahá'í Faith, Mirza Husayn 'Ali Nuri (1817–92), was a Persian Shi'a Muslim and a follower of the Bábist sect. Led by 'Ali Muhammad Shirazi, the self-styled Báb (gate), Babism prophesied the imminent return of the 'twelfth imam' to bring peace and order to the world. Over a period of about a decade, 'Ali Nuri came to realize that he was the fulfilment of the prophecy and, in 1863, declared he was that messenger of God, adopting the title Bahá'u'lláh, 'the Glory of God'.

Bahá'u'lláh claimed to be the most recent of a series of divine messengers that has included Abraham, Moses, Jesus, Muhammad and Buddha. He said these 'manifestations of God' were bringers of the word of one God with many names, in a form suited to a particular time and place. Central to his teachings are the ideas of unity, peace and understanding, and the elimination of religious conflict through mutual respect. He was imprisoned for his beliefs, but after his death the Bahá'í Faith spread from Persia worldwide, and today has an estimated seven million adherents.

The Bahá'í House of Worship
at Wilmette, Illinois

Cao Đài

Although not recognized as a religion in Vietnam until 1997, Cao Đài was formally established in 1926 and rapidly became the unofficial national religion of French Indochina. Spiritualism was popular at the time (see page 374) and, at a seance, three mediums – Pham Công Tac, Cao Quynh Cu, and Cao Hoài Sang – claimed to have communicated directly with God. They were entrusted by Đuc Cao Đài (the Highest Power) to establish a new religion with the aim of unifying all world faiths to achieve global peace.

Its full title, Đai Đao Tam Ky Pho Đo, means 'Great Faith of the Third Universal Redemption', the first having been brought by Judaism and Hinduism, and the second by Buddhism, Confucianism, Taoism and Christianity. Cao Đài is monotheistic, but as well as the creator, Highest Power, it recognizes a plethora of prophets and other holy people, such as Jesus, Muhammad and Buddha, but also less likely figures that include Julius Caesar, Joan of Arc, Shakespeare and Chinese revolutionary Sun Yat-sen.

Unitarian Universalism

Many new religions preach a message of inclusivity and respect for all religious beliefs, but none more so than the Unitarian Universalist (UU) Church founded in 1961. Unlike almost any other religious institution, it has no specific belief system or dogma, other than its commitment to a 'free and responsible search for truth and meaning', and respect for each individual's belief. Instead, it takes a largely humanist neutral stance, placing more emphasis on understanding than faith in a deity or belief in an afterlife, and spiritual growth rather than worship.

UU has its roots in two 19th-century Christian movements, the American Unitarian Association and the Universalist Church of America. Both had a strong tradition of libertarianism and respect for intellectual as well as spiritual freedom. As a consequence, UU embraces ideas from many different religions and cultures. Its members hold a wide variety of beliefs, and include a number of humanists, agnostics and even atheists who, nevertheless, feel the need for a spiritual dimension to their lives.

Cargo cults

Before the 19th century, the peoples of the Pacific islands of Melanesia, Micronesia and New Guinea had little contact with the Western world. But colonization – and especially an explosion of global trade – brought a sudden influx of Europeans and, with them, Western culture. Instead of adopting the Christianity taught to them by missionaries, however, the islanders incorporated Western values into their indigenous religions in a surprising way.

It was the material goods (understood as 'cargo') that had the greatest impact on them, for they took them to be gifts from their gods that had been hi-jacked by the white men. Some thought that these gifts would be restored to them and the colonizers driven out by a saviour, variously known as John Frum, Tom Navy or even Prince Philip. To propitiate the gods, followers of these so-called cargo cults devised rituals imitating the military drill of the Western servicemen, and constructed replica weapons, airstrips and even aircraft to attract the favours of the saviour.

Caribbean and Afro-American religions

African slaves in the New World were generally forced to adopt the Christian religion of their owners. But while those in North America tended to accept the new faith, those in the Caribbean and South America clung more fiercely to African beliefs and customs. Consequently, their descendants have practised several hybrid or syncretic religions, largely consisting of ancient beliefs with a thin veneer of Christianity – for example, disguising traditional spirits with the names of Christian saints.

Probably the best known of these is Vodou, which originated in Haiti under French rule in the 18th century. The name came from the Vodun religion of West Africa, but also incorporated ideas from the Yoruba religion, and French Catholicism. Variants of the religion developed in Spanish colonies, such as Cuban Vodú and Dominican Vudú. The influence of Spanish Catholicism can be seen in Santería (Worship of Saints), a syncretic Yoruba/Catholic religion practised in many Latin American countries, and the specifically Brazilian Creole religions, Candomblé and Umbanda.

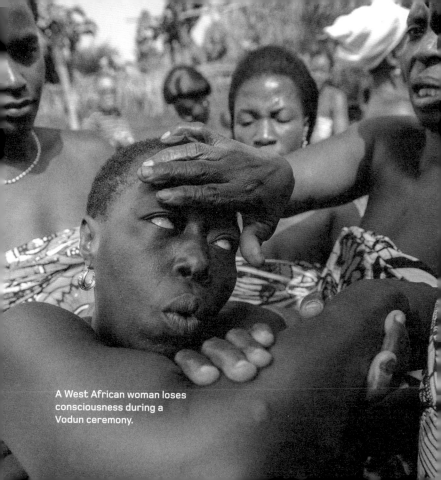

A West African woman loses
consciousness during a
Vodun ceremony.

Rastafari

An unusual Creole religion emerged among the Afro-Caribbean people of Jamaica in the 1930s, with almost no influence from traditional African religions. Instead, Rastafari merged some Christian concepts with a new mythology that emerged from New World Pan-Africanism, and the growing social and political awareness of people of African descent.

The Rastafari movement was sparked by the coronation of Tafari Makonnen (opposite) as Emperor Haile Selassie of Ethiopia in 1930. Revered as Ras (Prince/Duke) Tafari, from which the movement gets its name, he was seen by black Jamaicans as the prophesied Jah (Lion of Judah; the incarnation of God sent as a saviour). In the Rastafarian interpretation of the Bible, the Zion of the Old Testament is in fact Africa, and Babylon – the source of evil and exploitation – is the land of white Europeans. As much a cultural and political movement as a religion, and made popular by its association with reggae, Rastafari spread to Europe with the emigration of Jamaicans to Britain, and also into North America.

Unification Church

The founder of the Unification Church, Sun Myung Moon, was brought up in Korea in a family that converted from Confucianism to Christianity. With this perspective, he reached an unusual interpretation of the Bible, and believed it was his mission to complete Jesus's unfinished salvation of the world. To this end, he established what is commonly known as the Unification Church, in 1954, and twelve years later published *The Divine Principle* explaining the movement's theological basis.

In it, Moon reinterpreted the Christian story of Adam and Eve, blaming her spiritual attachment to Satan for the Fall, which condemned all their descendants to be born corrupted and sinful. Jesus had come to redeem humanity, but had been crucified before achieving the most important part of his mission, getting married. To bring about salvation, Moon exhorted his followers to follow his example and take or renew wedding vows in the Blessing ceremony of the Unification Church, often alongside hundreds of other couples.

Scientology

One of the most controversial new movements, Scientology has long been considered a cult, but is now officially recognized as a religion in several countries. It was the brainchild of science-fiction writer L Ron Hubbard, who in 1950 wrote the book *Dianetics: The Modern Science of Mental Health*.

Hubbard's original intention was to offer a new form of psychotherapy through a system of 'auditing', in order to clear a subject's mind from past trauma. The process, later aided by use of the electro-psychometer or E-meter Hubbard invented, took on a spiritual dimension, however, as dianetics became more about clearing the soul – known in Scientology as the 'thetan' – than the mind, and Hubbard founded the Church of Scientology on these principles. Adherents of Scientology progress through various levels of auditing, removing the subconscious memories from past lives called 'engrams', with the goal of becoming 'operating thetans' and thereby achieving a full spiritual understanding.

Nonbelievers

The existence of supernatural beings was once taken for granted, but as thinkers began to seek rational explanations for the world around them, some questioned the existence of such entities. However, the powerful role of religion in most societies – at least until modern times – meant that any such thoughts were regarded as subversive. In response to challenges to their faith, Christian and Islamic philosophers constructed rational arguments for the existence of God.

From the Renaissance onwards, the Church lost some of its political authority, and it became more acceptable (and less dangerous) to be openly atheist. Although sometimes pilloried for their ideas, 18th-century philosophers such as Voltaire and Immanuel Kant reopened the philosophical debate, paving the way for more militantly atheist thinkers. Among them were Ludwig Feuerbach (opposite, who famously declared that 'Man created God in his own image'), Karl Marx ('Religion is the opium of the people') and Friedrich Nietzsche ('God is dead').

AUG. NEUMANN.

Science vs religion

The accelerating pace of scientific discovery from the 16th century onwards posed a considerable challenge to religion. While Islam had encouraged scientific enquiry, the Christian Church saw it as a threat to its authority.

The Renaissance marked the beginning of a Scientific Revolution pioneered by the likes of Galileo Galilei, Andreas Vesalius and Francis Bacon. As Europe entered the so-called Age of Reason or Enlightenment, science and rational thought became increasingly valued and, among many thinkers, more so than religious faith. Science explained the workings of the Universe in mechanistic terms that required no supernatural intervention, and religions had to adapt in the face of the new evidence. On the other hand, science has been unable to explain all the mysteries of the Universe, or to answer existential and moral questions. Many of the most recent scientific discoveries and theories can seem almost mystical, perhaps posing more questions than they answer, and not completely negating the basis for religious belief.

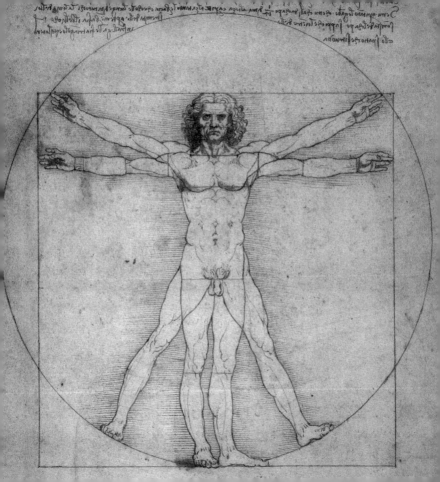

Agnosticism and atheism

People who lack a religious belief are by no means a homogeneous group. At one end of the spectrum of nonbelievers are those who find that religion simply plays no part in their lives, sometimes called apatheists. At the other end are 'strong' atheists who explicitly deny the existence of God. In between are a variety of 'agnostic' positions that essentially adopt an attitude of uncertainty.

Some of these agnostics have an inherently atheistic or theistic leaning, but are willing to be convinced one way or the other. Others have a more positive belief that we *cannot* know for certain. The philosopher Immanuel Kant, for example, examined the arguments and concluded that it is impossible to prove rationally the existence of God. Bertrand Russell later ridiculed the debate by asking for arguments to disprove his belief in an invisible flying teapot orbiting the Sun. A widely held view today sees religious belief a a matter of faith rather than reason, that therefore cannot be treated by rational argument.

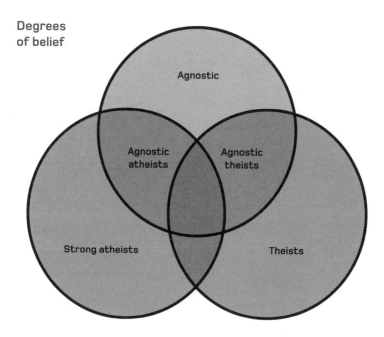

Degrees of belief

Agnostic

Agnostic atheists

Agnostic theists

Strong atheists

Theists

As well as those who firmly believe in the existence or nonexistence of God, there are others who simply believe that we cannot know. Among these agnostics, there are some who nevertheless either believe or disbelieve, but are willing to be proved wrong.

No religion at all

While strong atheists share an active belief in the nonexistence of God, there are nevertheless some among them that recognize the human need for some kind of faith. Some turn to established religions, such as Buddhism or Confucianism, that do not entail belief in a deity. Others belong to humanist organizations that affirm belief in the innate value of human beings and fulfil a community function traditionally provided by religious institutions, while denying a role for God.

Many others view religion as an outdated superstition or, like Marx, as a palliative offered by society to those who are suffering. And some are actively opposed to religion. Political regimes such as the communist governments of China and North Korea have seen it as inimical to their ideology, and banned or persecuted believers. Individual atheists ranging from the philosopher Ludwig Feuerbach to the scientist Richard Dawkins have also denounced religion in damning terms, describing it as, at best, an obstacle to progress and, at worst, as a form of indoctrination.

A Soviet political newspaper from 1929 calls for the replacement of traditional Christian festivals with new ones celebrating industrialization and state achievements.

The future of religion

It often seems that we are living in an increasingly secular society, particularly in the developed world. Most countries have secular systems of government, and few have an officially sanctioned state religion. Yet despite this, only around 10 per cent of the world's population describe themselves as atheist.

In fact, the vast majority of people describe themselves as religious, with most identifying with an established religion. And while in a handful of mainly northern European countries religious belief appears to be on the decline, most of the major religions report growing numbers of followers. There seems to be a continual revival of interest, and breakaway groups and new religions continue to emerge. Some scientists have suggested that we humans have a psychological or even biological or evolutionary need for religious faith. Devout believers explain the need for faith as spiritual, rather than scientific. Whatever the reason, the evidence is that religion is an intrinsic part of human life, and will remain so long into the future.

The US Presidential oath of office, sworn on the Bible, shows how even today, religion remains deeply ingrained in even the most avowedly secular of nations.

Glossary

Abrahamic religions
The three monotheistic religions (Judaism, Christianity and Islam), each of which claims the prophet Abraham as their common forefather.

Afterlife
The eternal life after death of the immortal soul. Most religions include a belief in some form of afterlife, often a specific place where the souls of the dead go.

Agnostic
A person who neither accepts nor denies the existence of God.

Animism
The belief that all living things possess a soul or spirit. In some animistic religions, even non-living things such as rivers and mountains are believed to have spirits.

Apocalypse
The final battle between good and evil, which in some religions heralds the End of Days or a Day of Judgement.

Apostate
Someone who abandons or renounces his or her religious faith, either completely or to convert to another religion.

Atheism
The lack of belief in a god. By contrast antitheism is active opposition to a belief in a god or gods.

Blasphemy
The act of insulting or showing contempt or lack of reverence for a god, holy people or sacred things.

Celibacy
Abstinence from sexual relations and/or marriage, often for religious reasons.

Covenant
In theology, a pact, commitment or contract between God and his people, involving mutual obligation. The word is generally associated with Judaism, and the agreement between God and the Jewish people.

Cult
A non-traditional religious movement. The term is often used pejoratively, and to describe pseudo-religious movements with dubious motives.

Deism
A theological position that believes rational observation of the natural world indicates the existence of a single creator.

Deity
Another word for god or goddess.

Denomination
A grouping or subdivision within a major religion.

Devil
The primary opponent of God in monotheistic religions. In some polytheistic religions, an evil destroyer god opposes the good creator god.

Dharmic religions
Centring round the concept of Dharma (meaning law, or duty), Dharmic religions originated in India and include Buddhism, Hinduism, Jainism and Sikhism.

Doctrine
The official beliefs and teachings of a religious group.

Dogma
In Christianity, the prescribed and unarguable doctrine taught by the church. The term is also used loosely to describe beliefs that are not supported by evidence or argument.

Enlightenment
1. In Buddhism, arriving at an awareness or knowledge of the cause of suffering.
2. The period in 18th-century Europe when the dogma of the Church was challenged by science and philosophy.

Fundamentalism
A controversial term describing certain Christian and especially Islamic movements advocating a return to extreme conservative religious and moral values.

Heresy
Opinions or beliefs that contradict orthodox religious doctrine.

Heterodox
Not agreeing with accepted beliefs, particularly in church doctrine or dogma. *See also* **Orthodox**

Humanism
A secular approach to morality and explanation of the world centred on human reasoning rather than divine inspiration.

Immanent

Present in the world. An immanent God encompasses everything in the world, or manifests himself in the world.

Incarnation

In Christian theology, the embodiment of God the son in human flesh as Jesus Christ. In Hinduism, several gods also had human incarnations known as avatars.

Infidel

Non-believer, not necessarily an atheist, but one who does not hold the same beliefs as the speaker. Similar pejorative terms are pagan, heathen, or kaffir.

Laity

The ordinary followers of a religion, as opposed to the priests.

Martyr

One who suffers death or punishment for upholding his or her religious beliefs.

Monk

A person who has devoted his life to the service of God, through prayer, worship and austerity. Women who similarly withdraw from society are called nuns.

Monotheism

The belief that there is only one God.

Mysticism

The belief that union with God, or a deity, is possible through contemplation and mystical experience rather than doctrine.

Omnipotence

All powerful. The deity of most monotheistic religions is assumed to be omnipotent, and may also be omniscient (all-knowing), omnipresent (present everywhere) and omnibenevolent (all-loving).

Orthodox

1. Conforming to approved church doctrine.
2. In Christianity, the eastern branches of the Church that split from the Roman Catholic Church.

Pantheism

The belief that God and the universe are identical, that all reality is divine.

Pantheon

A collective term for all the gods of a particular polytheistic religion.

Polytheism

Worship or belief in more than one god.

Prayer

The act of addressing communications to a god, either in praise, or to petition for his help or forgiveness.

Prophet
A person believed to be a divinely inspired messenger, who has received a message directly from God.

Reincarnation
The belief, common in Buddhism and Hinduism, that an aspect, such as the soul, of a living being is re-born in a different physical form after death, creating a constant cycle of life, death and re-birth.

Resurrection
The belief that the dead will rise again on the day of judgement. In Christianity, the term also refers to the resurrection of Jesus Christ after his crucifixion.

Revelation
Something disclosed or revealed, especially God's message to a prophet.

Saint
A holy person, especially one recognized as having an exceptional degree of holiness, or responsible for a miracle.

Scriptures
Sacred writings, believed to be the word of God, or have his authority.

Sect
A group that develops different beliefs or practices within a religious movement or tradition and separates from it.

Secular
Separate from any religion at all.

Shaman
A person thought to be able to commune with spirits or gods, and to act as an intermediary between them and humans.

Shrine
A sacred place, usually commemorating a holy person or holy event.

Syncretic
Combining or amalgamating different faiths or religions in such a way that the original features become blurred.

Theology
The systematic study of religious beliefs and God.

Transcendent
Existing beyond the world. A transcendent God exists outside the realms of the physical world, space and time.

Worship
The offering of adoration, praise and devotion to God, normally in communal ceremonies or rituals.

Index

Abraham 192, 194
Æsir 58, 60, 62
Afro-American religion 390
afterlife 14, 40, 60, 314, 362
agnostics 402
Ahura Mazda 66, 70
almsgiving (*zakat*) 324
amulets 188
ancient religions 36–64
Anglicanism 292, 294
Angra Mainyu 66, 70
animistic beliefs 30
Apostles 250, 252, 254, 256, 272
artha 88, 92
atheism/atheists 398, 402, 404, 406
atman 86, 104, 140

Bahá'í 382
baptism 266
Baptists 290
Brahma 104, 106, 112

Brahmins 102, 122
Buddha (Siddhartha Gautama) 128, 130–52, 158, 160, 170
Buddhism 14, 128–68
   bodhisattvas 150, 154, 156, 164
   Eightfold Path 24, 142, 144, 152
   enlightenment 146, 148
   Four Noble Truths 142, 144
   Indian roots 136
   life and teachings of Buddha 132–4
   Mahayana 164, 166, 168
   marks of existence 140, 142
   meditation 152
   Middle Way 138
   monks and monasteries 154
   nirvana 136, 148

   as a philosophy 158
   spread of 160
   temples and stupas 156
   Theravada 162, 164, 166
   Vajrayana 166
   Zen 168

Cao Đài 384
Cargo cults 388
Caribbean religions 390
Catholicism *see* Roman Catholicism/Catholic Church
Chinese religion 42–4, 170, 170–80, 380
Christian festivals 268
Christianity 240–300, 400
clergy 276, 332
Confucianism/

Confucius 128, 168, 170, 176–80
Creation stories 10

Daoism 168, 172, 174
dharma 80, 82, 88, 90, 98, 100, 136, 358
dissenting movements 298
Druidism 376

Egypt, ancient 38–40
Eucharist 264
Evangelicalism 300
evil 24

Falun Gong 380
folk religions 28, 34
future of religion 406

Ganesh 110
Gnosticism 370
gods/goddesses 12, 18, 20, 46, 48, 50, 54, 58, 104–12, 184
good 24
Great Schism 282
Greece, ancient 46–52
gurdwara 368

Guru Granth Sahib 356, 366, 368

Hades 46, 52
Hadith 316, 334
hajj (pilgrimage) 328
Happy Science 378
Hare Krishna 126
Hasidism 224, 226, 228, 230
heaven 178, 260, 262
Hebrew Bible 190, 192, 196, 206, 240
hell 260, 262, 314
Herzl, Theodor 234
Hinduism 14, 80–126, 136
  branches of 124
  cycle of rebirth 86
  deities and goddesses 104–12, 124
  festivals 118
  four *purusharthas* 88–94
  four stages of life 100
  nonviolence 98
  sadhus and gurus 122
  social classes (*varnas*) 102

temples 116
worship 114
holy people 22
Holy Trinity 258

indigenous religions 28–34
Islam 302–50, 400
  art and architecture 342
  clergy 332
  conservative and fundamentalist 348
  Five Pillars of 318–28
  Golden Age 310, 342
  halal food and drink 338
  paradise and hell 314
  prophets 304
  spread of 350
  women and 340
Islamic Empire 308

Jains/Jainism 72–8
Japanese religion 182–8, 378
Jehovah's Witnesses 298
Jesus 240, 242–56, 264
  birth of 244, 268

crucifixion and
resurrection of 246,
256, 268
disciples of 250
teachings of 248, 252
Jewish diaspora 202
Jewish identity 236
Jews, persecution of
234, 238
jihad 336, 348
jinas 72, 74
Judaism 190–238, 242
Ashkenazim 202, 228,
230
festivals 216
God's covenant and
the Promised Land
194, 196
kosher food 222
modernizing of 226,
232
Orthodox 226, 232
Patriarchs 192, 236
rabbis 210, 228
rites of passage
218
Sephardic 202, 230
service of the heart
212
signs and symbols 224

synagogue 214
and women 220

Kabbalah 208, 230
kama 88, 92
kami 182, 184, 186, 188
karma 82, 96, 136, 358
Khalsa 362, 364

Laozi 128, 170, 172, 174
Last Judgement 260,
262
Last Supper, The 254
Luther, Martin 286, 288

Mahavira 72, 74
marga 94
martyrs 270
meditation 120, 136,
152
Mesoamerican
religions 64
Mesopotamian
religions 36
Messiah 198, 242, 260
Methodism 290
Millerites 298
Mithraism 56
moksha 88, 94, 120
monasticism 22, 154

Mormons 296
Moses 19, 198, 204, 224
mosques 330, 342
Muhammad, Prophet
302, 304, 306, 308,
312, 316, 336

Nanak, Guru 352, 354,
362, 366
natural world 8
Neopaganism 376
New Testament 242,
252
nonbelievers 398,
402–4
Norse religion/
mythology 58–62

Orthodox Christian
Church 282, 284
Osiris 38, 40

Pope, the 276, 280, 282
Protestantism/
Protestants 270, 276,
286, 288, 292, 300
Puritans 292

Qur'an 304, 312, 316,
334, 340

Ragnarök 62
Ramadan 326
Rastafari 392
Reformation 286, 288, 290
Revivalism 300
rituals/rites 18, 26
Roman Catholicism/ Catholic Church 270, 274, 276, 278–80, 286, 290, 292
Roman Empire/Romans 54–6, 272, 282
rta 82

sacred places 20
saints 270
salat (call to prayer) 322
samsara 80, 86, 88, 90, 136, 144, 158
Santeria 390
science vs religion 400
Scientology 396
Second Coming 260, 262
secularism 406
shahada 318, 320
Shaivism 124
Shaktism 124
shamans 22, 32, 42

sharia 334
Shia Islam 318, 332, 344
Shinto 182–8, 184, 378
Shiva 104, 108, 110, 112, 124
Sikhism 352–68
   five Ks 364
   five vices 358, 360
   path to salvation 358, 360
   worship 366
Smartism 124
society and religion 26
souls 14
spirits/spirit worlds 14, 184
Spiritualism 374, 384
Sufism 346
Sunni Islam 332, 344
supernatural beings 12, 16

talismans 188
Talmud 206, 212
temples 50, 116, 156, 186, 188
Ten Commandments 24, 196, 204
Tenrikyo 378
Theosophy 372

Torah 204, 206, 208, 212, 222, 226
traditional beliefs 28
Tripitaka 134

underworld, Greek 52
Unification Church 394
Unitarian Universalism 386

Vaishnavism 124, 126
Vedas, the 84
Vedic religion 82, 84, 102, 136, 138
Virgin Mary 244, 278
Vishnu 104, 106, 112, 124
Vodou 390

Wicca 376
worship, act of 26

yin and yang 44, 174
yoga 120

Zionism 190, 224, 234
Zoroaster/ Zoroastrianism 66–70

Quercus

New York • London

Text © 2017 by Marcus Weeks
First published in the United States by
Quercus in 2017

Any member of educational institutions
wishing to photocopy part or all of the work
for classroom use or anthology should send
inquiries to permissions@quercus.com. Every
effort has been made to contact copyright
holders. However, the publishers will be glad
to rectify in future editions any inadvertent
omissions brought to their attention. Quercus
Editions Ltd hereby exclude all liability to
the extent permitted by law for any errors
or omissions in this book and for any loss,
damage or expense (whether direct or
indirect) suffered by a third party relying on
any information contained within this book.

ISBN 978-1-68144-168-9

Library of Congress Control Number:
2017931433

Distributed in the United States and Canada
by Hachette Book Group
1290 Avenue of the Americas
New York, NY 10104

Manufactured in China

10 9 8 7 6 5 4 3 2 1

www.quercus.com